CHURCH MUSIC AND THEOLOGY

by the same author

SCM Press
THE WISDOM OF THE FATHERS

Independent Press
I'LL PRAISE MY MAKER
ORGANIST AND CONGREGATION
THE MUSIC OF CHRISTIAN HYMNODY

Duckworth
THE CHURCH AND MUSIC

John Murray
HYMNS AND FAITH
HYMNS AND HUMAN LIFE

Lutterworth
THE GIFT OF CONVERSION

Herbert Jenkins
THE ENGLISH CAROL

Church Music and Theology

ERIK ROUTLEY

MUHLENBERG PRESS PHILADELPHIA

First published 1959
© SCM PRESS LTD 1959

Printed in Great Britain by
The Camelot Press Ltd., London and Southampton

CONTENTS

AUTHOR'S NOTE

PERHAPS the following tract can best be described as 'theological footnotes to musical criticism'. I doubt if it is much more. But for what it is worth I am bound to acknowledge that in its preparation I have been greatly helped by the recollection of the Church Music Seminar in which I was permitted to take part at the Study Conference of the SCM at Swanwick in July 1957. I cannot now possibly sort out which of the following ideas are mine and which 'belong' to other members of that group. None of them would care to be responsible for this, but none the less I must mention them with gratitude.

I ought also to say that I have used in chapter 5 a certain amount of material that formed one of the three lectures I was privileged to deliver on Christian Worship on the St Andrew's Foundation at Emmanuel College, Victoria University, Toronto, in November 1955.

E.R.

June 1958

ABBREVIATIONS

EH   *The English Hymnal,* Oxford University Press
AM   *Hymns Ancient and Modern: Revised edition,* Clowes
CP   *Congregational Praise,* Independent Press

CHAPTER ONE

PROLOGUE

THIS book represents a modest attempt to furnish prolegomena for theological discussion and criticism of church music. In our time church music is a subject widely discussed among a Christian public whose level of general musical instruction has been rapidly raised during the past two or three generations.

Musical moralism in church circles has correspondingly flourished. There have always been some who have taken churchmen to task for the low quality of music they tolerated in their worship. John Wesley did it. Pope Pius IX did it. John Antes La Trobe, in his *The Music of the Church* (1831) did it at leisurely length. Samuel Sebastian Wesley in those *Few Words on Cathedral Music and the Musical System of the Church* (1849) which run to seventy-seven pages, did it as a gesture towards better working conditions for his fellow church musicians. The author of the preface to Novello's *The Psalmist* (Vol. I, 1836) did it in order to sell his book. No musical generation since that of John Wesley has been without its moralists; and as for the ages before the Reformation, when music was still considered a proper province for theologians, the reader may find many examples of patristic and medieval musical moralism in Oliver Strunk's *Source Readings in Music History* (Faber, 1954), or, if he cares for a slighter book, in my own *The Church and Music* (Duckworth, 1950).

But it is characteristic of this age of easy communication that during the last fifty years the process has been greatly accelerated. Many manuals of church music for clergy, choirmasters and organists have found their way into print from the pens of such authorities as (to name only a few) M. F. Bell, Athelstan Riley, Sir Sydney Nicholson and Harvey Grace. Perhaps the best current book is C. H. Phillips, *The Singing Church* (Faber, 1947). Publications like *The Musical Times, Musical Opinion* and the *Bulletin* of the Hymn Society have devoted much space and effort towards imparting of information, the sharpening of scholarship and the 'raising of standards'. No hymn book is now considered complete except it be provided either with a full-scale historical Companion, or with some form of biographical index, and it is well known—it might almost by now be said, notorious—that hymnology is a field of study commanding a widening public.

Even those works which are primarily designed to give information are rarely free of critical judgment. But apart from the general manuals, we now enjoy the fruit of the work of such organizations as the Church Music Society and the Gregorian Association. We have had, in the field of plainsong, the scholarly and illuminating work of J. H. Arnold, E. T. Cook, W. S. Vale and others. We have had, in early polyphony, the definitive editions of E. H. Fellowes, and we are still receiving similarly definitive editions of Restoration church music from Mr H. Watkins Shaw. The various major denominations have formed musical associations with critical and instructional aims such as the Methodist Church Music Society, the Guild of Presbyterian Organists, and the Congregational Organists' Conference.

Beyond all these there have been the establishments of St Michael's College, Tenbury (1856), and of the Royal School of Church Music, which began in 1927 under Sir Sydney Nicholson as the School of English Church Music, and now serves the Anglican Communion throughout the world from its headquarters at Addington Palace, Surrey. Not a few non-anglican musicians have been influenced by it through its residential courses and summer schools, and non-anglican choirs have been, since 1955, granted association with it.

This is to speak, and only in a selective fashion, of what has happened in England. The same kind of thing may be said of America, where although the standards are different, the appointments more lavish, the hymn books more easy-going and the musical associations more numerous, the spirit of information is very widely active, and the spirit of informed criticism is by no means silent. Such figures as Winfred Douglas in the U.S.A. and Healey Willan in Canada have advocated the 'raising of standards' not without effect, and whereas the more popular musical publications in America may fairly be judged unequal in their quality, the recently formed School of Church Music at Whitby, Ontario, under the auspices of the United Church of Canada, shows, through its journal, *Jubilate Deo*, much sensitiveness to the complexities of church music criticism.

Nor are these activities confined to anglican and protestant churches. Roman catholicism has also its modern counterparts of the Cecilian societies, and is showing a new awareness of the necessity for avoiding the worst in musical composition and performance through the work of those who are following the spirit of Pope Pius X's famous *Motu Proprio* of 1903.

But in England the best source for information about the ideals prevailing in the upper stratum of educated anglican church musicians is in the two reports published by committees on church music set up by the Archbishops. The first of these, entitled *Music in Worship*, was published in 1922, and the second, *Music in Church*, in 1951 (revised, 1957). Although the Royal School of Church Music was not concerned, as an organization, in the compilation of the later document, and although its foundation document is the *Principles* set out by its founder, the 1951 Report may be taken as a very fair index to the ideals followed in that institution.

It would, then, be presumptuous to offer another manual of instructions and moralizings about church music. Existing books and institutions have excellently covered that ground. The only reason I have for attempting the present book is a conviction that there is work to be done by those who can bring to the study of church music a sense of theology. It is, of course, for others better educated than I in both disciplines to do this work. I can only suggest the lines along which it should go forward. To do it adequately will be to return to the Middle Ages, in music's nonage, when gifted theologians were not above turning their attention to the relations between theology and music, and proceed from there to a position which takes account of music's 'coming of age', but does not involve that failure of theological nerve which I hold to be at the root of our present disorders, and to imply a much greater threat to future church music than most of us are at present aware of.

I presume to think that in *The Church and Music* I adequately demonstrated the bankruptcy of that kind of theological criticism which is no more than semi-informed ecclesiastical restraint, grievance or suppression. I now address myself to the more contentious question whether the modern techniques of criticism by musicians and musical parsons are in any way more sufficient. I contend that although in modern utterances on the subject there is much urbanity, and much refinement, and although in modern practice there is a notable impatience with the pragmatic standards of the days of our grandfathers, there is still a lack of theological stiffening in all this thinking. It may be more than I can achieve, to bring to the sympathetic notice of the reader the necessity for re-enthroning theology as the queen of the sciences—and of the arts—but I must attempt it.

By a theological stiffening for our musical criticism I mean this. We are all aware of the moralistic tone that the institutions and books take with us, and equally aware of the resentful response which this evokes in people who call themselves plain men. The question I would put is, What content is there in the 'good' and 'bad' which you musical moralists imply in your judgments? Having myself committed a good deal of musical moralism in my time, I would here seek to provoke, by taking the part of *advocatus diaboli*, some reaction in the moralists which will lead to the deepening of our thinking—and, what is of more importance, to the opening of new ways of reconciliation between the artist and the cleric.

I ask the reader to note that I make no assault here on the more formidable question, 'What, in art, is goodness and badness?' That is matter for a larger treatise and a more capable author than you have here. I am concerned with the more circumscribed problem of that musical casuistry which we employ in the practice of church music. I am after the 'good' and 'bad' in the mind of a church music preceptor, and beyond that limited field I shall only rarely allow myself to stray.

By 'theology' I mean that ultimate speech about the nature and the works of God which is mankind's response, however halting, to God's revelation. I presuppose in 'theology' a credal system founded in the Scriptures, but not a literalist biblicism. I expect to find in Christian belief, derived from Scripture, clues to the right behaviour of musicians in church, but I do not think that we need be content either to quote Eph. 5.19 and to say on the basis of that text that all is well with church music, or to quote Amos 5.23 and say that the whole practice of church music is irrelevant to the true and sincere Christian life.

It is well—I insist on this—that musical education has made such great strides within the church. It is well that so much that is vulgar and unprofitable is now so widely resisted in the church. But if the vulgar and unprofitable be a devil, are we clear that his place will not be taken, or is not now being taken, by seven others of his kind less easily recognizable to our professionally polarized sight? What lies behind our 'vulgar' and our 'unprofitable'. Is this hymn tune vulgar because Vaughan Williams said it was? Is that liturgical custom unprofitable because they say it is at Addington Palace or Tenbury? None of those authorities would accept any such assertion for a moment. Implicitly they all look to Scripture and doctrine; but who will interpret them to theology by unwrapping some of their implications and analysing some of their axioms? That is what I here presume to attempt.

CHAPTER TWO

THE OLD TESTAMENT

'SINGING TO THE LORD'

IT is in the nature of things that people should want to 'Sing to the Lord', and the practices associated with religion in Old Testament times share with those associated with all religions in making provision for man's response to this commandment of natural law. The injunction 'Sing to the Lord', so characteristic of the Psalmists and other singers (e.g. Ex. 15.21; I Chron. 16.9; Ps. 68.32; 96.1, 2; 98.1; Isa. 42.10; Jer. 20.13, etc.), is less a demand for specific action than a signal that what has been waiting for expression may now be given it.

Those who want information about the history of biblical music will find it well summarized in chapter VII of the *New Oxford History of Music*, Vol. I (1957). I need not recapitulate that story here. But it is worth noting that the authorities who write in that source leave us in no doubt that the Scriptures, although they form our only source for what knowledge we can claim about the music of Israel, are in themselves a secondary, unreliable and almost accidental source. That is not surprising. The last thing that would have occurred to a Jewish writer under the Old Covenant is to write a history of music. For one thing, histories of that kind were a matter in which such writers took no interest; for another, music was to them so natural an activity as to be hardly susceptible at that stage of moral criticism: moral criticism of music, as we shall see, is in the Old Testament always criticism of the musician; and for a third thing, this is not their subject in any case. All we can gather from the Old Testament by way of direct evidence is that music was very widely in use in the culture of Israel at all its stages, from the primitive triumph-song of Miriam to the relatively sophisticated liturgical system of the Second Temple, and that this music was always sung and frequently accompanied by musical instruments. The nature of these instruments is, apart from the most generalized classifications, purely conjectural, and our opinions on it are based on no archaeological or historical evidence whatever.

As for the music itself, why, we can distinguish epics and dirges in secular contexts (in so far as any context for Israel was secular), and songs of praise, thanksgiving, instruction, personal experience and liturgical significance in the religious context. Professor Mowinckel has taught us of the august liturgical import of the 'Enthronement Psalms'; when we read the 'Psalms of Ascent' their text gives ground for a fairly clear reconstruction of the half-domestic, half open-air context in which they were used; linguistic evidences combined with attention to their content show us with reasonable plausibility the provenance of certain reflections on personal experience or on history, such as we find in Ps. 129 or Ps. 137; certain sidelights are thrown on popular musical habits by the appearance of such a lyric as that which opens Isa. 5. All this, and other studies of similar sort, indicate that music was never far from poetry, and poetry never regarded as wholly irrelevant to the imparting of that religious conviction which is the chief business of the Old Testament.

THE AXIS OF OLD TESTAMENT CRITICISM

But what is quite clear,—indeed, given any understanding of the sacred writers' purpose in the Old Testament at all, it is clear *a priori*—is that while any conclusions based on scripture concerning the history of pre-Christian music are bound to be highly conjectural, the Old Testament is an excellent source for moral teaching about its religious use. Here the Old Testament evidences are as clear and persuasive as their historical evidences are hazy and accidental. You do not read the Old Testament in order to ascertain facts of natural history any more than you read fiction in order to be informed about railways. But what the Old Testament is concerned with is the revelation given by God to his people, and the category within which this revelation is most often transmitted is that of morals. 'God's will and man's rebellion' is the normal polarity of Old Testament narrative, exhortation or song. Along these lines we may be certain of finding guidance.

There is, then, an *assumption* that religious men and women will respond to a call to 'sing to the Lord'. This assumption corresponds to the natural desire to sing which, being as natural as the desire to speak, and quite possibly more primitive, is in itself morally neutral. Comment on this appears explicitly in certain places in the prophets, and this comment is by way of warning people against the unrestricted or disobedient concessions that can be made to this non-moral desire. The moral content in 'It is a good thing to give thanks to the Lord, to sing praises to thy name, O Most High' (Ps. 92.1) is of the lightest. Nobody ever thought it was a bad thing. But the prophets now and again comment on religious music-making as characteristic of those habits of worship which bespeak a degenerate spiritual condition. The most unequivocal denunciation of religious music thus abused is in Amos 5.23-24,

> Take away from me the noise of your songs;
> To the melody of your harps I will not listen.
> But let justice roll down like waters
> And righteousness like a mighty stream.

This is almost paralleled, though not in respect of the musical reference, in Isa. 1.12-17; and Jer. 7.1-7 comes to much the same thing.

More numerous are prophetic denunciations of music as a symbol of secular triviality. Amos in one place audaciously introduces the name of David in such a context:

> Woe to those who lie upon beds of ivory,
>   and stretch themselves upon their couches,
> and eat lambs from the flock
>   and calves from the midst of the stall;

who sing idle songs to the sound of the harp,
   and like David invent for themselves instruments of music,
who drink wine in bowls
   and anoint themselves with the finest oils,
   but are not grieved over the ruin of Joseph! (Amos 6.4-6.)

And Isaiah similarly:

Woe to those who rise early in the morning
      that they may run after strong drink,
   who tarry late into the evening
      till wine inflame them!
   They have lyre and harp,
      timbrel and flute and wine at their feasts;
   but they do not regard the deeds of the Lord,
      or seek the work of his hands. (Isa. 5.11-12.)

From such passages we can infer in their writers an acute sense of the moral force of music. It was natural to them to seize on its symbolic properties, and to reflect in their denunciations a truth which Plato expressed in more measured terms, but in the end with less aesthetic insight, when in the *Republic* he denounced certain musical modes as agents of moral corruption.

Perhaps the single text in the Old Testament that reveals what would now be called musical sensibility is that in Ezek. 33.32-3, where the inattentiveness and sentimentality of the people towards the prophet's message is compared with the attitude of people who listen to a sweet voice and a seductive tune. Concert-goers who affect a certain kind of beatific smile and gushing comment, the bane of sensitive performers, are just what Ezekiel is thinking of, and any serious minded musician feels for him in a task about which both know something.

But the critical reader will rightly urge us not to lay too much weight on texts of this kind. After all, the passages from Amos and Isaiah which we have just quoted were written in Hebrew poetry, and may well have been actually sung. The *tu quoque* could have been directed at the prophet by a contumacious listener. By his rebuke against the corruption of music is uttered against a *corruptio optimi*. Music ought not to be an .tion, but it is made so by the repulsive incongruity be-its beauty and religious zeal, and the state of things in the slums.

What really matters to us is the moral content of that Law which early Israel regarded as God's moral self-revelation to his people. Not specific rebukes, but the principle behind all Old Testament rebuke, is what we must discover if we are to use the Old Testament scriptures as a guide.

Now there is an antinomian tendency in most pious Christians, encouraged by a mis-reading of certain very familiar passages in the Gospels, which encourages the belief that little edification can be gained by a Christian from the Jewish Law. The Pauline doctrine of 'The Law' as a dispensation from which a man 'in Christ' is released is never at any point so expressed as to mean that the law written in the early books of Scripture is to be disparaged; none the less, Paul is often regarded as authority for disparaging the law in Exodus and Leviticus. The same comment applies to the Epistle to the Hebrews. Above all, it most certainly applies to Matt. 5. Here a casual recollection of the chapter suggests to many people that our Lord said, 'The law told you this: but I, contradicting it, tell you the opposite.' Not at all.

LAW AND GOSPEL

The great series of antitheses in Matt. 5.21-48 are thus introduced:

You have heard that it was said to the men of old, 'Thou shalt not kill. . . .' (21)

You have heard that it was said, 'You shall not commit adultery' (27)

You have heard that it was said to the men of old, 'You shall not swear falsely' (33)

You have heard that it was said, 'An eye for an eye. . . .' (38)

You have heard that it was said, 'You shall love your neighbour
and hate your enemy' (43)

Of these the first three contain quotations from that summary of
moral law which we call the Ten Commandments (Ex. 20). Our
Lord's comment in each case is that mere avoidance of error, or of
technical breach of the law, is an insufficient aim for his disciples.
The fourth is a quotation from Ex. 21.24, a passage susceptible of
much critical comment. The immediate context of this application of the *lex talionis* is the highly specialized case of injury sus-
tained by a pregnant woman in consequence of a brawl; but
commentators are prepared to say that although it appears at
this point, it is applicable to all the cases of injury mentioned in
the preceding verses. Whatever may be the truth about the text,
it is difficult to suppose that our Lord in speaking, or the evangelist
in reporting and collating several of his speeches, would pass so
abruptly from precepts of the moral law of universal application to
a comment on one fairly remote clause in the statutes of ancient
Israel. Obviously what he means is, 'Your habit of thinking is,
"an eye for an eye, a tooth for a tooth" '. He flatly denies this
habit of thinking in a manner in which he does not flatly deny the
quotations from the Commandments.

The transition to the fifth clause then becomes quite smooth.
'You shall love your neighbour' does indeed stand in Lev. 19.18.
But 'you shall hate your enemy' stands nowhere in Scripture.
What our Lord here directly denies is again a common habit of
thought. If any law of the land were based on it, he would deny
that as well; but the point here is that he did not *deny* the law as
written in Scripture. With all his force he denied the pharisaic
and popular interpretations of it, and with all his force he empha-
sized the necessity of doing more than merely avoiding breach of it.
But in The Law as his fathers according to the flesh understood it,
in The Law as God's moral self-revelation, he never saw anything
but an object of veneration.

We have already suggested, anticipating what we shall argue in the next chapter, that the essence of the moral teaching of Christ is that it is not enough to be blameless, that blamelessness will not save. And that, as we shall see, will form a cardinal point in our present argument. But it is worth our while to observe one more way in which the Old Testament before we fully take into account the New Testament, can enlighten us.

THE PRINCIPLE OF RESTRAINT

Although it must be agreed that the old Law is largely expressed in the form of prohibitions, it cannot have escaped a careful reader of the Law that it is unlike any other legal system in its ruthless abhorrence of a certain kind of human pride, self-sufficiency, and meanness. Much of the law, of course, contains rough justice of the kind that to some extent persists in modern society. The death penalty is appointed for crimes of which murder is only one (though murder is distinguished—Ex. 21.12f.—from other kinds of killing). A domestic life, a view of marriage, is presupposed from which we may fairly say that Christianity has delivered us. Admitted—and yet consider such injunctions as these:

> If you meet your enemy's ox or his ass going astray, you shall bring it back to him. If you see the ass of one who hates you lying under its burden, you shall refrain from leaving him with it. You shall help him to lift it up (Ex. 23.4-5).

> When you reap the harvest of your land, you shall not reap your field to its very border, neither shall you gather the gleanings after the harvest. And you shall not strip your vineyard bare, neither shall you gather the fallen grapes of your vineyard. You shall leave them for the poor and the sojourner. I am the Lord your God (Lev. 19.9-10).

> When you make your neighbour a loan of any sort, you shall not go into his house to fetch his pledge. You shall stand outside, and the man to whom you make the loan shall bring the pledge to you. And if he is a poor man, you shall not sleep in his pledge (i.e. the coat which is the only pledge a poor man can offer, and which serves him also for a blanket); when the sun goes down, you shall restore to him the pledge that he may sleep in his cloak and bless

you; and it shall be righteousness to you before the Lord your God (Deut. 24.10ff.).

The second of those passages chimes sympathetically with another (Ex. 23.10f., cf. Lev. 25.1-7) in which the Israelite is commanded to plough and sow his land for six years, and for the seventh to allow it to lie fallow, 'that the poor of the people may eat' (Ex. 23.11); this is called in Lev. 25.6 the 'sabbath of the land'. Despite the august association of the 'sabbath' in Ex. 20.11 with the finishing of the Creation, its social importance lay in its inducing a habit of desisting not only from work as onerous, but from work also as profitable.

'This shall be righteousness to you before the Lord your God'; this technique of self-restraint, implying self-abasement, is what will, says the sacred legislator, put you right before God, will enable you to share responsibility in God's design for the world. It is hardly too much to say that behind this precept is the notion that this self-restraint in mankind is the only thing that will correspond to the self-restraint which is God's own technique in creating and bearing with the world.

It can further be said—and indeed I here propose to treat it as settled—that when our Lord resisted 'the law', he was primarily resisting those interpretations of it which had drained off from it this irrigation of generosity, and attacking those disciplines which, having lost the saving aim of mercy, were now nothing but means to that very pride which was the Law's primary target.

It is recognized from the earliest stages of religious consciousness in the Old Testament that the archetypal sin is pride. In ordinary practice the defence against this sin is a principle of restraint, a principle that you have no proved right to all of what is lawfully yours. All Old Testament morality could be arranged along this one axis—that you must renounce part of what you are entitled to. There is a direct line from Leviticus 19 to Philippians 2. In the Old Testament we have a negative and partial expression of that positive and total doctrine of grace which is so firmly insisted on in all New Testament teaching.

21

I now make bold to apply this principle to music, and particularly to church music. It is a principle that applies universally. Corresponding to God's omnipotence is a freedom in man to love God by choice, or to hate him. Corresponding to God's limitation of his omnipotence in creation, is man's primary moral duty to renounce his tithe. Corresponding to God's creative faculty is a creative faculty in man (who, however, cannot create *ex nihilo*) and in the exercise of that faculty man is called to renounce what corresponds to the form of absolute omnipotence which God has renounced. Good doctrine teaches that God's omnipotence, vis-à-vis his creation, is not absolute. Neither are man's rights over what he, in his own lower way, has created.

I think that it must be tacitly understood in aesthetics that there is something sufficiently approximate to a personal relation between a man and what he has artistically created, and between a man and what other men have in this sense created, to warrant our extending to aesthetics the principle of the limitation of omnipotence. It is perfectly clear that we are obliged, however great the constitutional power we allow to a King or President or Government, to require that governing person or body to limit its power. Between persons the exercise of absolute omnipotence is a major blasphemy. In the aesthetic world it is not a blasphemy, but it is quite certainly an error that has far-reaching consequences, and, what is more, an error which if we can here expose, we shall be exposing only just in time to prevent malefactions of a kind as disastrous as they may be unexpected.

CHAPTER THREE

THE NEW TESTAMENT

WE will assume, then, that the primary 'Thou shalt not' in the Old Law is 'Thou shalt not be proud'. In the New Testament there is no reference whatever to music, apart from certain heraldic references in the singing of the heavenly hosts in the Book of Revelation, and one or two stray references in the Pauline epistles to the singing of hymns and spiritual songs (Eph. 5.19, Col. 3.16). While plenty of comment is possible on such passages, neither they nor any others tell us anything specifically about the making or use of music.

But if we penetrate beyond the letter to the principle, we have as much guidance, and of the same general kind, as we can get from the Old Testament. What we must here especially attend to is the principle of Grace as distinguished from the principle of Law.

In another place (*The Gift of Conversion*, Lutterworth Press, 1957), I have attempted to expose this principle. I there demonstrated to the best of my ability that the principle is implicit in the Old Testament and explicit in the New. I have already here referred to the principle that blamelessness will not save. This is adumbrated in the Old Testament, but it is the very life-blood of New Testament moral teaching. There is, to put it briefly again, one world in which the best you can achieve is the avoidance of error; there is another in which that is the least that is expected of you, the best being an indefinite extension of positive good, or grace. It is error, according to the bye-law, to go less than one mile with the man who obliges you to carry his pack; but what is the good of going only one mile? What is the positive *good*? The second mile is more than a repetition of the first: it is a different kind of action. You can expect a startled acceptance on the oppressor's part of your act of *grace*, where before you had only a routine acceptance of your fulfilment of the *law*.

Not to expend space on an extensive recapitulation of what I have elsewhere written, I would summarize the New Testament principle of Grace thus:

1. Grace is here used to mean a whole dimension of living, of which 'the second mile' is an illustration in one specialized moral field.

2. The notion of Grace is diversified over the whole range of human activity and consciousness, until it is fully apprehended that the state of the Christian soul that lives fully in the Kingdom of God is a state I have described as 'welcoming the duty'. That is, without any abrogation of man's right and duty to make free moral choices, to a man 'under grace' what God wills for him and what he *wants* are in the end the same. That way alone lies that 'blessedness' (Matt. 5.3-12), or simply, happiness, which a man in Christ may legitimately seek and find.

3. It is God's design that the whole universe shall consciously live 'under grace'; that the obedience which man owes to God in the moral field shall be reflected in all the other fields, including the physical; and that man's cheerful, chosen obedience to God shall result in a loving, self-restrained dominion over those things which in the order of things have been placed 'under him', which in turn will produce a corresponding cheerful obedience from them to him. Towards such a consummation the creation groans and travails.

4. Therefore 'in the kingdom' men are unconcerned with *a certain kind* of 'judgment' (Matt. 7.1). Judgment considered as fault-finding is of no interest in 'the kingdom'. It is just not on the agenda. Live on the principle that judgment is fault-finding, and you will have, and engender in others, a vision of God as a fault-finding judge, an examiner on the watch for mistakes (Matt. 7.2). It is for this reason that we do not get from Jesus short answers about the 'rules' of the kingdom. Leviticus tells us, or told Israel

(and corresponding legal systems can tell us) what must and what may not be done. In the teaching of Jesus we are told only the kind of thing that happens in the context of the kingdom. Certain primitive notions of practical justice are at once upset (as in the parable of the labourers in the vineyard, which is not a directive for economists but a picture of grace at work); certain differences of 'merit' are as indistinguishable 'in the kingdom' as difference of distance are indistinguishable to a man looking at a line of objects with his eye trained *along* that line. 'The law' still holds, of course; a man 'in the kingdom' may not commit adultery (to say he may is the error of antinomianism); the man 'in the kingdom' is not exempt from the law that enacts that bad drains bring disease. But as for the drains, he regards it as his religious duty, not simply as a placation of the goddess Hygeia, to devise good drains: and as for adultery, what concerns him is not avoidance of adultery but the achievement of either felicitous marriage or sanctified virginity.

Now I do not wish to say that this shows a new method of aesthetic criticism. I say rather that this is the unsuspected paradigm of the principle of aesthetic criticism which has been assumed as long as fully developed criticism has been in being. Serious musical criticism, outside the church, has always taken for granted the fulfilment of 'the law', and gone on to assess how much positive good was achieved in this composition or in that performance.

An example or two will indicate what we mean. There is a 'rule' in the composition of music which directs that the progressions known as 'consecutive fifths' and 'consecutive octaves' are forbidden. The following is an example of its breach:

The music-student, working 'under the law', is taught to avoid that. If he cannot yet 'hear' that the progression makes an ugly sound, then he must take the word of his teacher that it does. But as he goes on to study music he will discover that quite a number of musicians are happy to break this 'law'. He will also discover that this 'law' applies only to music of a certain kind, using a certain vocabulary, and not to all music whatever.

For example, he will come across this phrase in a published work for voices:

He will see that the vocabulary of the piece as a whole is the same as that within which 'fifths' are forbidden. But there they are, and very agreeable they sound. And then he will run into almost any work of Vaughan Williams and find that parallel fifths and octaves are not merely a special effect, but are an integral part of their very texture, because the composer uses another vocabulary. All the time he will be aiming at the faculty for writing music in which the avoidance of ugly 'fifths' will never be a vexatious placation of a law, but will be the natural thing to do: in which he won't *want* to write fifths that make the kind of sound you hear in Ex. 1.

Consider, then, the position of a professor of harmony glancing over Ex. 2, or over a work of Vaughan Williams (verisimilitude will demand the assumption that Vaughan Williams is a new and unknown composer at this point), and suppose that examiner says, 'Those are consecutive fifths: therefore the phrase is wrongly written. They must come out.' Of what does that remind us? Why, it reminds us of the Pharisees interpreting the sabbath-law in such a way as to make reprehensible the rubbing out of ears of corn (Mark 2.23). And just as the Pharisees' legalism was capable of much more disastrous perversions than that, so as to make it reprehensible for Jesus to heal on the sabbath, so the legalism that divorces the prohibition of 'fifths' from the under-lying principle of symmetry and proportion which it is designed to express, can radically ruin musical judgment and, what is more, ruin the musical faculty of the learner. To compare such issues is to associate the very small with the very great: but the pattern is identical. It would be absurd to contend that professors of harm-ony are as frequently in error as were the Pharisees in our Lord's time; the professors have, after all, less at stake than the Pharisees had. What is important, however, is to show that a simple Gospel principle has as a matter of mere fact been accepted by the musicians (and all other artists) as a matter of course.

That is an example of elementary legalism. As for criticism, if you read any responsible judgment of a professional performance or of a new composition, nine tenths of it will be devoted to the question of how much good was done, and of what opportunities for doing good were clearly missed. Should the virtuoso play wrong notes, the critic will take him to task for it; should the composition be musically illiterate, the critic will not overlook that. But the avoidance of wrong notes is expected of the player, and illiterate music is not normally published, even for use in church. The usual kind of criticism follows the pattern of what I here select at random from a well known gramophone record review whose critical standards are high and whose editors are sparing of their praise. The work under discussion is the First Symphony of Brahms, and versions by two different conductors are being compared:

> Without question, A's is the finest Brahms C minor now in existence on a gramophone record. This is . . . orchestral playing of the highest distinction. . . . Compared with this, B's version seems dull and cold—efficient no doubt, but not a jot more than that . . . (E.M.G. *Monthly Letter*, December 1957, p. 3).

The difference between A's performance and B's, in the judgment of the writer of that review (which may or may not be right) is, so to put it, that A goes the second mile, and no doubt a third and a fourth, while B drops the pack at the thousandth pace. How much is added to legal blamelessness—that is virtually always the question. That is how musical criticism in general is carried on, and the point which I hope is here established is that in aesthetics a Gospel principle is assumed which places the moral judgments of aestheticians at once on all fours with those of advanced theologians.

I doubt, then, if this chapter achieves any more than the provision of a basis of irenical relations between artists and theologians. But if it does that, it will be something not inconsiderable.

We have now, however, to turn back to the legalism of the ecclesiastical moralists of music, to compare it with the libertinism which it is their desire to restrain, and to see whether a positive theology of church music criticism can yet be come by. To that end we must first examine two outstanding concepts which are familiar in this field of discourse: that of 'beauty' and that of 'romance'. Then we must make a further theological statement about the church. Then only shall we be able to offer some practical suggestions.

CHAPTER FOUR

BEAUTY

CERTAIN phases in the controversy between the church and the artists present a perplexity and an astonishment to those who overhear it from outside both worlds. While at some periods the church has been a munificent patron of art, at others it seems to have carried the restraint of art to the point of a positive cult of the ugly. In this special field of music we have the whole matter in a perspective which does not apply to the other arts, since music is, among the arts, a 'late developer', and those periods which witnessed the church's most generous patronage of art were those in which music was still in its infancy. But in a general way we may recall what seems to be the malignant hideousness of so much nonconformist architecture, and the whole puritan suspicion of visual aids to worship which has conditioned so much of our modern English church life. We may recall the remarkable fact that a certain kind of 'zeal for souls' is accompanied by what sensitive people regard as a debased taste in music and ecclesiastical décor. And with all that we must face the persistent generosity with which the church has for many generations now offered hospitality to the second rate. We recall Percy Dearmer's famous attack on the commercial and spiritual second rateness which he saw in the church of his day (about 1900), in the introduction to *The Parson's Handbook* (7th edition, O.U.P.); 'A modern preacher often stands in a sweated pulpit, wearing a sweated surplice over a cassock that was not produced under fair conditions, and holding a sweated book in one hand, with the other he points to the machine-made cross at the jerry-built altar, and appeals to the sacred principles of mutual sacrifice and love.'

There at once is a clue to the moral implications of ugliness, expressed in the phrases and thought-forms of an age now past, but none the less for that based on an abiding principle. I quote it at the outset in order to arouse a sense of the complexity of the whole matter of beauty in worship.

But to attack the question as near the root as we can, we must begin with the quite unquestionable, if not very palatable truth that 'beauty' is not a New Testament word. The word 'beauty' appears nowhere in the King James version, neither, in the Greek, does the word *kallos*, or the word *euprepeia*, or any word that can mean 'beauty', appear in any sense but the strictly moral. Indeed, 'beauty' in the post-romantic sense is a totally unbiblical word. In the King James Version of the Old Testament 'beauty' translates no fewer than nine Hebrew roots; but in every case the meaning is limited to a quality, and is never allowed to move over into an abstraction. 'Beauty' is not a thing any Hebrew could have found himself seeking as an end in itself, even though it is a quality which, along with other qualities, he was prepared to ascribe to such objects as deserved it. The most famous of Biblical texts on beauty, beloved of preachers at choir-festivals, 'O worship the Lord in the beauty of holiness' (Pss. 29 and 96) means no more than 'Worship the Lord with decent ornaments'—something (as one might expect, knowing the vital concreteness of the Hebrew tongue) a good deal less abstract and romantic than what we usually take that text to mean.

We must leave to the next chapter a discussion of what 'romance' means, and of what is the Christian answer to the need expressed in that notion. For the moment we keep to this: that while the New Testament talks of charity and of truth, it does not talk of beauty. Therefore the biblical theologian will not want to use language that suggests that 'beauty' is an autonomous or absolute category.

We can summon help at this point from St Thomas Aquinas, where he says, (*Summa Theologica*, Ia IIae xxvii 1) that the beautiful is that of which the apprehension itself is pleasing (*cuius ipsa apprehensio placet*), or, elsewhere, that which being contemplated pleases (*quod visum placet*). That is a definition of the beautiful, not a description of the mechanics of contemplating the beautiful, and it will not stand weights for which it was not constructed. But it bears this important comment: that for St Thomas, the beautiful is neither something wholly objective, nor something wholly subjective: it is not something existing in its own right, to be sought in its own right; nor is it something having its existence wholly in the eye of the beholder, and therefore about which no general proposition can be made. Being contemplated, it pleases. It exists enough to 'please', but not enough to 'please' without being contemplated.

And whom does it please? The definition is not designed to answer that. But the short answer is—it pleases a sinner. Nothing could be more obvious, and yet rarely is the consequence of that platitude taken into account. It brings us, however, at once to our second main proposition here, which is this: that there is no hideous conventicle, no ghastly religious daub, no miserable hymn or demoralising hymn tune, no mawkish anthem or organ voluntary, no spiritually depressing piece of church furniture, but somebody has thought it beautiful. Beautiful, I insist—not merely serviceable. All these things are adornments of worship, or they are supposed to be so. Nobody will call a building ugly if somebody did not before call it beautiful.

Pause on this. It is the puritan strain in English religious life that has been most often accused of cultivating the ugly. But such a generalization needs careful qualification. What is really offensive about the ugliest manifestations of post-puritan church architecture is its content of pretentiousness; the pretentiousness implies that behind the façade there is an insufficient backing of truth and honour. In practice, it implies a combination of large and impressive size with cheap materials, and with an implied contempt for craftsmanship. There are very few Puritan meeting-houses of the first generation left now: but those that do remain are not at all to be described as ugly: what they are is modest—dull, perhaps, uninspired, but never ugly in the pretentious sense. They avoid pretension as easily as they avoid the rhetorical impressiveness of a medieval cathedral, simply because their builders have no theological use for either.[1]

But when you come to the building that is really appalling, why, you must admit at once that it was deliberately made so, and that what is appalling to you was beautiful to its designer. If he did not call it beautiful, he would have used some other word like 'fine' or 'impressive', meaning that it was more than merely useful: that it not only *did* something but also *said* something.

When we come to church music we discover a tendency to pretentiousness which becomes first noticeable after the Restoration—perhaps Purcell's Te Deum in D is the earliest example of it—and obtrudes itself more offensively as we move nearer the year 1900. Something disastrous has happened to the aesthetics of post-Reformed Christians to permit this. We here merely note the fact that without any doubt at all it did happen, and return

[1] In some cases, of course, it can be, and ought to be, put more offensively than this. Some forms of ugliness come direct from the sin of greed. Two quotations from widely diverse sources may stimulate further thought along this line.

'Well, the point here is not social reform or the rottenness of capitalist culture. The point is that the whole world has got it firmly fixed in its head that the object of working is to obtain as large an amount of material goods as possible, and that with the increased application of science and the increased use of machinery that amount will be very large indeed, while at the same time the amount of necessary labour will become less and less, until, machines being minded by machines, it will be almost none at all. And the point is that this frame of mind is radically un-Christian and anti-Christian.' (Eric Gill, *Autobiography* (Cape, 1940) p. 281).

'The machine has aroused an ever-increasing yearning for speed, for frenzied accomplishments. There exists a psychological relationship between *speedomania* (frenzied swiftness) and ruthlessness . . . The machine forces results prematurely . . . The machine is the denial that progress has to grow within us before it can be realized outside ourselves. Mechanization takes away the belief in mental struggle, the belief that problem-solving needs time and repeated attempts. Without such beliefs, the platitude will take over, the digest and the hasty memorandum' (J. Meerloo, *Mental Seduction and Menticide* (Cape, 1957), p. 212).

A great deal of what we call 'Victorian ugliness' comes from the period when what is here criticized was in its approved infancy. Speed as a symptom of greed was probably its cardinal sin.

to our warning that at present there is no reason why it should not continue to happen.

But we may now state the third proposition of which aestheticians in church should take note, which is that no artist who really knows what he is doing would find much intelligible content in the notion that he tries to *make* his work beautiful. Here is a picture, or a piece of music, or a cathedral, that sweeps us all into ecstasy by its sheer beauty. It is not perhaps quite fair to say that to its maker the picture presents itself as a series of blobs of paint, or the music as a series of marks on paper, or the church as a heap of stones. But any artist who has mastered to any degree the very arduous business of translating his conception into communicable form will tell you that the process of *making* involves very little thought, if any, about beauty. So far from its being a part of his making-activity, attention to beauty in the thing being made is one of the major temptations which the artist must set aside. For beauty, as we have seen, is associated with the transaction between the thing being made and the contemplator. It is an effect which the artist hopes (perhaps prays) that he may achieve. But if he attempts to seek it in itself, to 'make beautiful' his piece of music or picture, he will probably disfigure it. While he is *making*, it will not seem to him a beautiful thing growing under his hand, but, more often than not, a recalcitrant thing which it is all he can do to keep on its designed track. Thus to express what happens in the process of *making* is probably to attribute to the thing being made a kind of conscious will which it does not have; it is really a way of saying that the artist is himself torn two ways as he makes— between the necessity of *right* making and the temptation to attend to the effect of the thing made.

This is not the place to take very far these thoughts about aesthetics in general. But it is within the terms of our brief to say that although the artist has a right, as it were, to the satisfaction that the making of a thing which others will accept as beautiful will give him, this of all rights he must not snatch at. He must resolutely and ascetically set all thoughts of it aside. When Miss

c   33

Dorothy Sayers wrote of certain perversions of artistic techniques in her illuminating book, *The Mind of the Maker* (Methuen, 1941), as illustrating perversions of the doctrine of the Trinity, she was illustrating our present point when she wrote of 'spirit-centred' art—namely, that which attends too much to its effect on the contemplator. I think that in the sphere of music, among composers of the romantic period, the one whose work shows most conspicuously the signs of structural distortion consequent on an insufficient resistance to this special temptation is Rachmaninoff. To quote two eminent examples of distortion in the work of a composer who at his best was a craftsman of great excellence, the structure of the last movement of his Third Piano Concerto is thrown clean out of proportion by the enormous and fantastic episode in E flat, supported almost throughout on a tonic pedal, which lasts from sections 48 to 58 (Hawkes Pocket Score, pp. 87-104);[1] and I fancy that something of the same kind has happened in the *Lento* section of the E minor prelude for pianoforte, Op. 32 no. 8, where everything is held up for a long inverted pedal on B which introduces ravishing sounds without advancing the argument an inch.[2] The former example is the more disastrous from the structural point of view in that its foreground material is taken from a subject that has already been used extensively in the first movement of the same work: a failure of idea has quite certainly been the occasion of the composer's taking refuge in beauty-hunting.

It is a consciousness of the elusiveness of beauty and of the dangers of hunting it that makes aestheticians write as does, for example, J. E. Barton, in *Purpose and Admiration* (Christophers, 1932) when he admirably says that 'discussions about sublimity are the very worst beginning for an orderly appreciation of art' (p. 252). A little later he writes thus, in the general context that the maker of a poker is as much entitled to artistic appreciation and subject to artistic asceticisms as the painter of a picture:

[1] The composer's recording is H.M.V. CSLP520.
[2] Recorded by Moira Lympany, Decca LXT2580.

Hegel once said that 'an old woman likes a sermon full of texts she knows, so that she can nod her head wisely when she hears them.' This might be a parable of our commonest attitude to the art of the painter. It is an attitude which ignores largely, if not wholly, the principles we ought to have learnt from the art of the pokermaker. It ignores the cardinal fact that a good painter, like a good poker-maker, sets out to give us something new, something he had made himself, and something which has for us the double value of perfection and freshness (p. 253).

It is interesting to compare this with another statement of St Thomas's about beauty, upon which Maritain comments in his *Art and Scholasticism* (Sheed & Ward, 1939, pp. 24ff. and 159). 'For beauty three things are required: in the first place, integrity or perfection (*integritas sive perfectio*), for whatever is imperfect is *eo ipso* ugly; in the second, proportion or harmony (*proportio sive consonantia*); in the third, *clarity* (*claritas*); for there is a splendour in all objects that are called beautiful' (*S.T.*, I xxxix 8). St Thomas's words are untranslatable, especially *claritas* and *nitor* (here rendered 'splendour'). But I suspect that Mr Barton's 'newness' takes up part of the sense of *claritas* and *nitor*, which certainly mean more than simply 'bright colour', and that his 'something of himself' is the only category not covered,—and this for obvious reasons, since he is not writing a primarily psychological treatise—by St Thomas.

At any rate, it is *design* that is paramount in the scholastics; you will get your *nitor* if you attend with care to *proportio sive consonantia*; and attending to them will take you all your time. Maritain (*ibidem*) compares Augustine's *splendour ordinis* and *unitas forma pulchritudinis* (Augustine, *De Vera Religione* 4); and wherever you touch the medievals you find them healthily free of any kind of false 'sublimity' in their discussions of beauty.

We may observe in passing, what we shall later have to consider in greater detail, that Mr Barton's 'newness' is a very large part of that area in the artist's work which falls under what we have already called the Gospel-principle. We shall find that one of the important questions to ask about a piece of music, and even about a piece of church music, is 'what in this is new?' Our judgment will in the nature of the case have to be on the Gospel plane, and not in the legal plane.

But for the moment we must follow where our present argument is clearly leading. What is this preoccupation with 'sublimity' that bedevils our thinking about art, and about music, and about church music? The popular name given to it is 'romanticism', and we will now turn to an investigation of what that means.

CHAPTER FIVE

ROMANTICISM

'ROMANTIC' is, among reforming church musicians, a primary adjective of opprobrium. Perhaps if you want to hear the word pronounced with the highest content of venom, you should hear it from the lips of a modern reformed pastor in Switzerland, speaking German. But in order to state just what we mean by 'romantic', and what is the theological answer to the defects of 'romanticism', it will perhaps be instructive to recall what Professor C. S. Lewis wrote some years ago in the Preface to the second edition of his *Pilgrim's Regress* (Bles, 1943) on this subject, which turns out to be the chief subject of that illuminating allegory.

Romanticism in literature is categorised by Professor Lewis in seven forms—(1) the dangerous or adventurous; (2) the marvellous; (3) the titanic and larger-than-life; (4) the abnormal or anti-natural; (5) the egoistic, inward-looking or subjective; (6) the rebellious in respect of civilization and convention, and (7) the sensitive to natural objects, associated with 'solemnity and enthusiasm.' He might well have said that the very famous lines of William Blake beginning 'And did those feet in ancient time' present in themselves most of the traits of romanticism in letters, and that our modern use of them with a splashy tune by a very fine English composer is a capital example of romanticism in practice.

He goes on (pp. 7f.) to speak of romantic experience in terms of (8) intense longing which *in itself* is prized for an object whose attainability is impossible, or at any rate beside the point, and (9) a sense of mystery in the thing longed for.

Now Professor Lewis is an acknowledged master of English

37

studies and a very able Christian apologist and moralist; but he is not a biblical theologian, and I do not think that he designed, in that categorization of romanticism, to give us clues to the understanding of Old Testament religion. But it really is impossible not to be struck by the precision with which he has given us a spectrum of natural human needs to which romanticism provides an illusory answer and the religion of the Bible a real answer.

We can summarize the Christian answer to 'romanticism' in a sentence: Christian doctrine substitutes eschatology for romanticism. But it would be fairer to present that proposition as a conclusion rather than as a premiss. The argument which leads to it takes us again into the Old Testament.

'Eschatology instead of romanticism' is what really disposes of categories (8) and (9) in the series above. Where 'romanticism' has a great longing for a distant object, which longing is in itself more real than the object and more satisfactory (as is supposed) than the object would be, Christian doctrine introduces the whole category of hope. The longing is not rejected, but fully admitted: it is often expressed as a personal longing for heaven, and thus it appears in many famous hymns, like the *Hora novissima*;[1] but it is there also in the 'groaning and travailing' of Romans 8.22. But the object longed for, though mysterious, is to Christians the most real thing of all: the personal enjoyment of the Beatific Vision, or the consummation of the Kingdom (Rev. 11.15). So real is it to the Christian consciousness that the Book of Revelation is constantly under fire from those who find it too concrete and particularized in its symbolic pictures of the Heavenly City.

But the whole Christian system of the New Testament is prepared by the developing religious consciousness of Israel recorded in the Old, and here we hear again and again the deep notes to which 'romanticism' was trying to find, without a Christian system, an answering chime.

Without straining matters an inch out of true, we can express it

[1] EH 371, 392, 412 and 495: the most celebrated English hymn taken from it is 'Jerusalem the golden'.

thus. Professor Lewis's first category is that of adventure and danger: that is exactly how the early Israelites were taught to look at life, through the archetypal allegory of the Exodus. A certain kind of 'security' was forbidden to them. The technique was worked out, with much pain and grief, in the great trek of the Exodus; but when Nehemiah would remind a later generation that the benefits of a settled civilization might turn out to be poison to the roots of their religion, he ordered that the sense of pilgrimage of the Exodus be symbolically revived in the Feast of Tabernacles (Neh. 8).

Man's capacity, indeed his need, for wonder (category 2) is adequately covered by the august sense of God which was native to Israel from the earliest times, and which is archetypally symbolised in Sinai. The sense of the titanic and the sense of the abnormal (3 and 4) are answered in primitive religion by the people's consciousness of heavenly and demonic agencies, angels and devils, which certainly left them with very little need to invent any more. As for the egoism and introversion that are characteristic of so much romantic literature (5), they represent a need which is met in the Israelites' sense of vocation: and the revolt against conventional civilization is sublimated in their sense, at their best, of being in this world but not of it, and in the prophetic rebukes both of the foreigners' idolatries and of the Israelites' own backslidings which are so familiar all through the story.

As for Nature (7), the most obvious and familiar of all the 'romantic' categories, nothing in the Old Testament is more impressive than the sensitive insight which brought Israel, at its most perceptive, between the Scylla of pantheism and the Charybdis of gnosticism. Nature to them is not God, but natural objects are very decidedly vehicles of the Word of God. Out of primitive tree-worship and hill-worship they brought the insights that we associate with the 'holy mountain'—holy not in itself but because God spoke from its height, and the great stones of commemoration and sancity, like Beth-el and Ebenezer, which reminded future generations of the presence of God.

39

The Old Testament is so nearly romantic. Indeed, it is in one sense romantic precisely in its incompleteness. For the heart of the Old Testament religious consciousness becomes in the end the Messiah, the hope of the race: and never was the 'romantic' delusion more completely and decisively acted out than in what Israel did when its Messiah actually came. Here was what they had hoped and lived for, and their reaction at every level was, just like that of the romantic, according to Lewis, if he ever did lay hands on the thing longed for, 'this is very disappointing.'

All this prepared the way for Christian doctrine: so that the complete answer to the needs exposed in all life, and partly met in the Old Testament, is there. It is there in the finality, in what has been called the 'realized eschatology' of the Christian revelation. Romanticism is rebuked and healed there. In as much as it loves the longing more than the achievement, it is rebuked, because the Revelation is the achievement. In a sense, what the spirit of adventure and the spirit of wonder are yearning for is achieved, and they have no more to long for. Yes: but this does not extinguish them. It is the differentia of the Revelation surely, that what is achieved is really more satisfying than the longing to achieve it—

Ubi non praevenit rem desiderium,
Nec desiderio minus est praemium.[1]

It is found in the end to be sin to love the longing more than the thing: it is Israel's sin. It is to reject the Revelation if we love thinking about angels and devils, and imagining them and inventing them, more than making friends with the angels and fighting the devils to whom now a name and a local habitation is finally given. It is a sin to love the egoism more than the courage and new being which defensive egoism was always aiming to achieve (and if I may here refer to chapter 10 of *The Gift of Conversion*, I need not pause here to amplify that). Nature is redeemed, and seen to be redeemed, through the sacramental principle, and 'All

---

[1] 'Never they crave, but their boon hath been granted,
Never that boon leaves their hope disenchanted' (*tr.* R. A. Knox).

things are yours, for ye are Christ's, and Christ is God's' (I Cor. 3.22-23).

Why then did romanticism, as Professor Lewis expounds it, come into action at all? For the simplest and most obvious of reasons: namely, that an age without a Christian anchor had followed an age in which these old, pre-Greek, pre-metaphysical Christian categories were accepted by those ordinary people from whom our artistic stock sprang. Romanticism is an anarchic and disobedient consequence of faithlessness. You could almost call it an anarchic and disobedient reversal of medieval *romance*. Historically, when you look and see from which countries the 'romantic movement' sprang, that is a self-evident fact. What, after all, is Blake, one of the authors of romanticism, but a one-man religion, a self-generated religious and philosophic system, full of that longing, that rebellion, that sensitiveness to human need and affirmation of human *being* which any educated man ought to have, and for which the religion of the Bible provides at every point?

We must now attend to the very important fact that romanticism in music, and therefore by derivation romanticism in church music, is in itself a peculiar phenomenon. Once again we have to remember that music is, among the arts, a 'late developer'. By the time of what Professor Lewis in another place calls 'the great divide' (he writes thus in his Inaugural Lecture, *De Descriptione Temporum*, Cambridge, 1955) music was about to reach the point of self-consciousness reached by painting in the fifteenth century. The consequences of this are of great importance, and if we neglect them our judgment of what the church has done with music will go astray. Painting and architecture, letters and sculpture, had all come to maturity by the Reformation: in England, at latest, letters had reached maturity by 1550. What the church of post-Christian society is to do with these arts, then, is the question what it is to do with arts fully matured, arts which can be seen to have been usefully and edifyingly employed by the church in other ages even though in later ages they were employed to less profit.

41

But with music, the situation is that the maturity of the art comes virtually within the post-Christian period. There is an enormous ambiguity—a heaven-sent ambiguity—about the place in history of J. S. Bach, to whom we shall have to pay special attention. But the general view is very likely to be that all music of maturity, being inextricably mixed up with the romantic rebellion, is useless to the church, and that the church's place of repentance must be historically prior to the achievement of that maturity.

Hence, as I suppose, the very commonly heard view that church music must, to save its soul, go back to plainsong, or go back to the Tudors; the assumption that church music 'fell' in a way comparable to the fall of Adam, some time in the eighteenth century, somewhere between Bach and Beethoven (or, as Karl Barth would no doubt hold, between Mozart and Beethoven, which is, between 1795 and the date, 1797, of Beethoven's Opus 1).

Assumptions of that kind—not, of course, thus crudely expressed as we normally meet them—we must here impugn. Altogether too much is normally made of the difference between Chopin (for example), as a romantic, and Bach, as a classic. What matters enormously, however, is that we fully understand what is at the heart of romanticism, and how the contemporary case against it should be prepared.

CHAPTER SIX

J. S. BACH

THE ARCHETYPAL BACH

THE literature on Johann Sebastian Bach is, as everybody knows, copious and erudite. This brief chapter seeks to make three special points about him which bear on our argument; it attempts no more than that. These points are (1) that the influences which Bach assimilated and humbly allowed to work on him are different absolutely from the influences which he himself exerted on those who came after him: this makes him a pivotal and unique and watershed-like figure in musical history; (2) that Bach uniquely combines the medieval craftsman with a mastery of modern musical rhetoric, and (3) that Bach has, with astounding results, suffered a romantic revival from which we are now being delivered in secular music but which we still allow to exercise influence in sacred contexts.

First, then, a word on Bach's influences, prior and posterior. There is something uncannily appropriate in the historical position which Johann Sebastian occupies. His life—1685-1750—stands astride the period at which all that is characteristically 'modern' began to come to life. His life was almost half done when Louis XIV died. In the remarkable family of Bachs covering the years 1520 to 1809 he stands almost exactly in the middle. (In *Everyman's Dictionary of Music*, ed. E. Blom, Dent, 1946, he stands twenty-sixth in a chronological list of fifty-three Bachs). All this is pleasantly symmetrical; but behind it there is a series of solid musical facts of great importance.

Ernest Newman, in his article on Bach in the *International Cyclopaedia of Music and Musicians* (Dent, 1942, pp. 91ff.) wrote thus:

Bach is the supreme exemplification of the thesis that the greatest artists do not so much originate as fulfil; the supreme confutation of the notion that an artist's greatness reveals itself in the extent to which he 'expresses the spirit of his age.' He was neither at the head nor in the ranks of any contemporary 'movement'; he originated no new form; he was almost as completely without influence on the half-century that followed his death as if he had never been born.

On the other hand, a little later, he writes:

He was the only composer in his own day, before him, or after him, who was able to use to the full, in practice, the theoretical possibilities of his art.

That sufficiently places him. The vocabulary was all there, waiting to be used; the vocabulary of pure polyphony not yet to be set aside as antiquated, the vocabulary of monody now sufficiently developed to carry something weightier than light opera. J.S.B. becomes therefore a contrapuntist worthy to stand beside Tallis and Palestrina, and a writer of melody to whom Schubert had nothing to teach.

The 'lack of influence' to which Mr Newman refers has as its efficient cause the plain fact that in his own lifetime nobody knew about J.S.B. apart from the courts and congregations among whom he worked. During the 'half-century that followed his death' we gather that Mozart accidentally discovered a few of his pieces, and that Beethoven in 1810 unsuccessfully applied to Breitkopf for a copy of the *Crucifixus* of the B minor Mass, because its ostinato bass would provide a good exercise for one of his noble pupils. The St Matthew Passion was revived by Mendelssohn exactly a century (1829) after it was composed. All this is familiar enough; but it is of importance, as we shall see.

But another contrasted point is worth adding here, namely, that while Bach humbly admitted his complete debt to his predecessors in all matters concerning form and vocabulary, and while his influence in those spheres on his successors is negligible, there is another sense in which Bach, in respect of rhetoric and subject matter, is archetypal for all music succeeding him down to

44

Brahms. I believe it could be shown that along certain important lines the 'romantic' composers have nothing to add to Bach. They invent new forms: they exploit new tonal combinations; but until we come to the impressionists, the modern atonal geometricians and the neo-medievalists, the whole school of symphonists and virtuosi owes everything to Bach.

Consider, for one example, the fashion of writing series of preludes in every key. Characteristically, Bach wrote his two sets of Preludes and Fugues to demonstrate the virtues of Equal Tonality, and thus to lend a hand to a modern and at the time not very popular development in musical mechanics. But after him come Chopin, Rachmaninoff, and the earlier, romantic, Scriabin. To them, such a series of pianoforte preludes is not a demonstration but something more like a confession of faith. Chopin and Rachmaninoff, at all events, summarize themselves with remarkable completeness in their series. They lay down in them the pattern of their technical vocabulary and their schemes of key-colour. But so does Bach in his: and he is the first to do it. Moreover, if you take a general view of Bach's '48', you surely find that they are, without intention and without, perhaps, any thought of conscious derivation, the archetype of all piano technique for the next 150 years. Pianists know well that he who can play the '48' has under his hands a comprehensive series of 'studies' for any kind of music up to 1900. Passage-work, cantilena, cantabile, passionate rhetoric: Chopin, Liszt, Schumann, Beethoven are all there in embryo, although neither Bach nor they knew it. You could argue along the same lines about his orchestral and vocal works. No new language comes for a century and a half, only new virtuosi of a specialized kind, and Bach alone shows himself to be master of the whole field.

This has much to do with our second proposition. Bach is in himself an extraordinary combination. He is in one way a child of his age, inasmuch as he fits quite peaceably into the prevailing fashions of church musician and court musician. There is at no point any sign in his music, whatever may have been his day-to-day sentiments, that he is a rebellious social misfit. At Arnstadt, Muhlhausen and Leipzig he is an organist: very well, he writes for the organ. At Cöthen he is a court musician: he writes secular music. At Weimar he is a choirmaster—then, obviously, he must write for his choir and for the august ceremonies of the Thomaskirche. He writes eighteenth-century music; he does not affect antiquarianism. He is perfectly content to do what this world requires of him. And he is that because he is among musicians the last of the medieval craftsmen. He is the most detached of all musicians from any preoccupation with what effect or influence his music will have. He is the most unromantic and matter-of-fact of workmen. He is not a great figure of tragedy, a frustrated, Byronic, melodramatic figure asking to be taken up by some Hollywood producer and made into a legend. He is an ordinary middle-class tradesman in music, an ordinary middle-class churchman: middle-class because he is of the eighteenth century, but tradesman and churchman because he is spiritually independent of his time, independent of ambition and lust for influence.

BACH AND PIETISM

One of the ways in which he accepted with an entirely peaceable mind the limitations of his place and time was in the matter of religion. Not only did he accept Christianity and grow up faithfully in it: he accepted the particular brand of Christianity which was purveyed in the places where he lived, which was, broadly, pietism. And pietism is a precursor of religious romanticism.

Pietism has many forms. Initiated by P. J. Spener with his foundation in 1670 of the *Collegium Pietatis*, and with the publication in 1675 of his *Pia Desideria*, it was a movement of evangelical revival typically consequent on the religious slump of the period of the Thirty Years' War. Thus summarized in the *Oxford Dictionary of the Christian Church*, *Pia Desideria* called for six points of revival: (1) Intensified Bible study; (2) A fuller exercise by the laity of their spiritual priesthood; (3) emphasis on the practical rather than the intellectual side of Christianity; (4) manifestation of charity in religious controversy; (5) a heightening of the devotional content of theological studies, and (6) the reform and revival of preaching. In modern terms this adds up to a fundamentalist outlook, a layman's religious movement, a contempt for the academic and cerebral aspects of Christian practice, a stress on interdenominationalism, a preference of prayer over instruction, and a system of conversion. It is not unhelpful to an understanding of Bach's religious background to note that he was, to all intents and purposes, moving among, and faithful to, groups of loyal adherents of the Inter-Varsity Fellowship; for that is exactly what, in its day, pietism was. If ever there was a limitation whose acceptance in J.S.B. was heroic, it was surely that of the libretti which he was called on to set to music in his *Passions* and in the sacred cantatas. One recalls (as Mr Basil Smallman has told us in *The Background of Passion Music*, SCM, 1957, pp. 13ff.) that he had much difficulty in getting hold of any tolerable libretto for the *St John Passion*. But what he got in the end is a series of meditations which, as soon as they break away from Scripture, are, as everybody knows, very heavily weighted on the side of natural personal grief, and quite innocent of any rejoicing in the Resurrection. Indeed, the pattern of his great choral works shows the effect of pietism on his work. We have the Passion story set in the versions of three of the Evangelists (the St Mark version has disappeared, and the St Luke, sometimes attributed to him, is spurious), always on a very large scale. The Resurrection gets much hastier treatment: his most considerable treatment of it is Cantata 4, *Christ lag in Todesbanden*,[1] an unusually ferocious and dramatic piece of work, with, as William Scheide points out, all its emphasis on the line in the text, 'It was a strange and dreadful strife'. By comparison, both the *Easter Oratorio*[2] and the *Ascension Oratorio* (otherwise called Cantata 11)[3] are lightweights. An examination of that exceedingly interesting pamphlet of William Scheide, entitled *Johann*

[1] Recorded, Nixa BLP311, Archive APM14046.
[2] Recorded, Vox PL8620.
[3] Recorded, Columbia LX3006, Nixa LLP8034.

Sebastian Bach as a Biblical Interpreter (Princeton Pamphlets no. 8, Princeton, 1952), and especially of the list of Biblical texts set by Bach on pp. 37ff., shows how strong is the pietistic influence.

Bach's apprehension of Scripture has no element of subtlety or of paradox. It is foreign to him, and to the tradition in which he wrote, to bid us 'rejoice in the Passion'. There is no setting in his works of Hebrews 12.2. He never sees the Passion as part of the story that leads to the Resurrection. And if it be tolerable to argue, with Geiringer (Karl and Irene Geiringer, *The Bach Family*, Allen & Unwin, 1954, p. 232) that the placing of what we call the 'Passion chorale'[1] at the beginning and end of the *Christmas Oratorio* is an indication of Bach's preoccupation even at Christmas time with the Passion (a questionable interpretation), why then this shows that, with the pietists, if there is one outstanding emphasis in their preaching, it is the Atonement.

Because he is essentially a craftsman, working in music without thought beyond the work, Bach's involvement with pietism made no difference whatever to the quality or texture of his music. We should here raise very serious doubts as to the sufficiency of the pietistic approach to the Faith: but nobody who does so can possibly claim any corresponding insufficiency in Bach's music. In Scheide's admirable phrase (p. 17), there is 'no music with more solid earthbound vitality' than Bach's. The very limitations of pietism he turned to God's praise; for the repudiation of subtlety involved a repudiation of poetry, and produced inevitably a naïf libretto which if it has nothing else to be said for it does at least refrain from attempting anything more than a lyric virtue; and libretti which show discontent with that limitation present special and sometimes intractable problems to a composer.

One other small matter must be noted here. Pietism, with its emphasis on congregational participation in worship, was much given to hymns. Its greatest poet is Paul Gerhardt (1607-76), whose hymns show pietism at its noblest;[2] some of them are known

[1] EH 102.
[2] English translations of Gerhardt include 'Commit thou all thy griefs' (CP 487) and 'O sacred head' (CP 127).

in translation to English congregations. Bach, with a characteristic
blending of the new pietism and the ancient dramatic technique of
'bringing the audience on to the stage' which is familiar in the
medieval Mysteries, interpolates chorales for congregational
singing in the narrative and meditation of the *Passions*. I want to
show a little later what an extraordinary, unexpected, and in places
disastrous influence this technique has had on later church music
practice. It is one of the most mysterious paradoxes in the story
of this most paradoxical of musicians. For the moment I merely
recall, what I have ventured to amplify in chapter 11 of my book,
The Music of Christian Hymnody (Independent Press, 1957), that
in his settings of these tunes Bach exemplifies all at once the heart
of his musical 'archetypalness'. The melodies themselves are old
and familiar: as familiar to his congregations as 'When I survey
the wondrous cross' is to Englishmen and Americans. But the
settings of them are entirely in an eighteenth century style:
broad, courtly, and impressive, harmony and counterpoint substituted for unisonal irregular rhythm, choral technique substituted for the peasant folk-song style of Luther's day. Nowhere
do we see better than here Bach's utter refusal to be anything but
a child of his own age. Here is no denial of history, no fugitive
archaism. This was the obvious thing to do for those people at
that time. This is no place to make educational gestures towards
the raising of their taste by insisting on original versions. This is
how, in this setting, hymns will naturally be sung. I do not know
whether, after a look at the chorales in the *Passions*, it is necessary
to say any more about Bach's self-forgetfulness and innocence.
It is not necessary to attribute these to him as costly virtues. We
do not say that he achieved this against the stream of what fashionable musicians were doing, or of what the church was demanding
The fact that the Passions are entirely unliturgical, and therefore
a break away from the original form and purpose of musical
Passions as they were conceived in the days of William Byrd, is no
evidence of rebelliousness, but precisely evidence of acceptance,
on Bach's part. Pietism was unliturgical. The supremacy of Bach

is precisely in this quality of 'acceptance' which it was given to him to exemplify in history.

BACH AND THE ROMANTICS

But now to our third proposition, which is that Bach, by one of the great ironies of musical history, suffered in due time a romantic revival. This has now, thanks to the arbiters of modern musical taste, begun to pass into history. But it is quite certainly a fact of history. We may briefly refer to this romantic revival of Bach, this revival of Bach as rhetorician, as master of musical effects, under the following heads.

In the first place, Bach became familiar to a couple of generations through the practice of arranging his works for musical media other than those for which he wrote them. In itself this could not have offended him; he was himself one of the world's great arrangers. But the tendency, probably invented by Liszt and certainly put about by his pupil Tausig, was to arrange his works in a style more impressive and less reticent than his own. The long series of large-scale organ works arranged for concert performance on the pianoforte contains in itself several comments on history, one of which is that works for the organ are (*a*) such that normally you must go to church to hear them; (*b*) not always played when you go there, because (*c*) in Bach's case they are very difficult to play. But, says the listener, they are enjoyable, especially when played on a large nineteenth-century organ. Then let us recapture this impressiveness, and transcribe them for the pianoforte in such a manner that their difficulty will certainly not be concealed from the audience, and their performer's reputation therefore will not suffer. And so we have Tausig and Busoni and others on the organ works, giving them a 'concert' ethos which is purely romantic—a 'larger-than-life', hero-worshipping ethos, which is as far as may be from the strictly 'chamber-music' atmosphere for which they were designed. A similar romanticism can be seen in the smaller arrangements of chorale preludes and cantata movements. Dame

Myra Hess some time ago arranged for piano the Adagio in A minor from the organ *Toccata, Adagio and Fugue* in C; in her arrangement, which insists always on reproducing a 16-foot tone in the bass (and at one or two points certainly reproduces sounds which Bach's harpsichord could not have made, since its extreme death was 16-foot F) Dame Myra has subtly altered the 'cool' climate of the original to a 'warm' climate, innocence to sophistication, austerity to richness.[1]

We may further recall the orchestral arrangements of organ works which used to be very popular—Respighi on the *Passacaglia* and Elgar on the *Fantasia and Fugue in C minor* used to be much in vogue. There is also the tendency to treat Bach like Handel, and to assemble choruses of enormous size and organs of vast resources for his interpretation. The conspiracy to make Bach a concert-hall draw has been now halted by the advocates of the baroque organ, the harpsichord, and the chamber orchestra and choir. Whatever may have to be said either way concerning their re-searches and interpretations, which remain controversial, it cannot possibly be doubted that the explosion of the spurious Bach myth of grandeur and rhetoric is clear gain in our time. To one aspect of this we shall have to return later. What we here contend is simply that this archetypal musician, and archetypal church musician, was honoured with the unique vocation of single-mindedness, equipped with a fully developed musical vocabulary, and alone of all musicians since 1600 an example of that 'accept-ance' which in our own sophisticated days has become a lost virtue. What we also contend is that delusions of grandeur and magnificence in the cause of church music are decidedly not to be fathered on Bach, but are part of the conspiracy of admiration to which he has been subjected by the romantic generation.

[1] Another familiar example of 'romantic' Bach-arrangement is Busoni's arrangement for pianoforte of the choral-prelude 'Ich ruf' zu dir', included in Lipatti's piano recital recorded on Columbia CX1386. All is well, and quite orthodox, until the repetition (unintended by Bach) of the final eight bars of the piece an octave lower (certainly unintended by Bach), finishing with three quiet but dramatic chords which are clearly designed to 'convey the feeling' of the piece.

CHAPTER SEVEN

THE BODY

JOHANN SEBASTIAN BACH, then, was an eminent example of
the literal observance of the biblical commandments to the musician. Much of what a musician has now been taught to regard as his
right, he renounced; that he was little tempted to do otherwise
and that his renunciation was made possible and even natural by
his temperament and circumstances is not to the point, for we are
not conducting an investigation into the personal virtues of
musicians. But if ever a musician can be said to have lived out
the Old Testament's implicit prohibition of self-interest and its
implicit injunction to self-denial it was he. It can further be said,
on the evidence of our fourth chapter, that the main weight of the
case against unregenerate romanticism is its discouragement of
this virtue, and, at some points, its positive encouragement of the
corresponding vice.

We must now go a little deeper into doctrine. Our last chapter
has brought us, as it were accidentally, face to face with a religious
system which has clear limitations, and which can degenerate into
spiritual self-interest more rapidly than any other. We showed in
what ways J. S. Bach was able to make a virtue of its weakness.
But having encountered pietism, and assuming the rightness of our
criticism of it as a sectional and partial Christian system, we must
now say on what positive principles we believe the church's
authority vis-à-vis the musician to rest.

We must fairly admit that the church is entitled to criticize the
musicians; and that church music is subject to a kind of criticism
from which music outside the church is exempt. It would be
ridiculous to suggest that there is one standard for the sacred and
one for the secular. Church music has enjoyed 'benefit of clergy'

for long enough, and has become ridiculous in the eyes of musicians at large because of it. But while church music is not dispensed from the ordinary requirements which music in general must meet, it stands also under the discipline associated with its being used to further the aim of worship. It is always used in a context in which its performers are not exclusively and its hearers not even primarily concerned with music in itself.

It may then be assumed that a musically-informed church authority and a theologically-informed musical authority can between them work out a counterpoint of criticism and precept in these matters. That is what such bodies as the Royal School of Church Music, whose staff contains both musicians and priests, are seeking to do. But without prejudice to any view of the present effectiveness of such bodies, we must state on what grounds we believe that such judgments should be made; and it is here proposed to state them in terms of a doctrine of the Church.

What is, as I believe, fundamental to a right understanding of our obligations here is to understand what is the connection between 'church' in the expression 'church music' and Christ, who is the Head of the church. St Paul roundly states that the connection is so close as to be expressible in the phrase, 'the body of Christ'. By far the most comprehensive and able linguistic study of the word 'body' in that expression is to be found in J. A. T. Robinson's book, *The Body* (SCM, 1952), and another indispensable book in this context is Father L. S. Thornton's *The Common Life in the Body of Christ* (Dacre: Black, 1949). Careful pondering of both those studies is here advised for any who would follow further the line of argument suggested in these pages of ours.

Here I am disposed only to say this: that the immediate context of the classic phrase, 'the body of Christ' as it appears at the end of Eph. 1 is of the greatest importance for the discovery of a right doctrine of behaviour and principle in all church matters. The writer of that Epistle (whom I assume, regarding evidences adduced to the contrary as inconclusive, to be St Paul) is concerned throughout that prodigious sentence which forms Eph.

1.15-23, to assert the lordship and victory of Christ, vindicated in the Resurrection.

> I do not cease to give thanks for you, remembering you in my prayers, that the God of our Lord Jesus Christ, the Father of Glory, may give you a spirit of wisdom and of revelation in the knowledge of him, having the eyes of your hearts enlightened, that you may know what is the hope to which he has called you, what are the riches of his glorious inheritance in the saints, and what is the immeasurable greatness of his power in us who believe, according to the working of his great might which he accomplished in Jesus Christ when he raised him from the dead and made him sit at his right hand in the heavenly places, far above all rule and authority and power and dominion, and above every name that is named, not only in this age but also in that which is to come; and he has put all things under his feet and has made him the head over all things for the church, which is his body, the fulness of him who fills all in all.

It seems to be the Apostle's purpose to show that faint-hearted rural deanery at Ephesus that the heart of their 'calling' is in the Resurrection; that they are 'one' with him to whom all this power was given through his Resurrection. In another place he shows similarly that the church thus intimately shares in the humiliation and death of Christ through baptism (Rom. 6.1-11), and elsewhere again he expresses his personal hope for a share in the suffering and Resurrection of his Lord (Phil. 3.10). This doctrine is well put by Professor T. F. Torrance (quoted in Daniel Jenkins, *The Strangeness of the Church*, Gollancz, 1956, p. 74) who wrote in the *Scottish Journal of Theology* (1949), 'Surely the essential form of the visible church wherein she images her Lord is to be found in her humble service in which the great reconciliation already wrought out in the Body of Christ is lived out among men, and the Church in life and action becomes, as it were, sacramentally correlative to the life and passion of Jesus Christ'. That is one of the many things that the apostle clearly meant by his phrase, 'the body of Christ', and it is precisely this that concerns us here.

For while Paul was writing to a local church, or group of churches, in some doctrinal difficulty, and Professor Torrance was writing observations on the ecumenical conference of the World Council of Churches at Amsterdam, the principle is perfectly well to be applied in our corner of the field. The gift of God to the church is this union with Christ; it is therefore to be expected of the church that in all matters of behaviour it will show forth the humiliation and the Resurrection of Christ. Many writers have applied this in other moral fields; but why should church music be dispensed from this grace?

Taking our stand on Professor Torrance's ground, and demanding that church music be 'correlative to the life and passion of Jesus Christ', what can we further say? What, on the face of it, has music to do with the suffering and the victory of Christ? It has much to do with it when we remember that music cannot be made at any level without the co-operation of sinners who are redeemed by that suffering and Resurrection, but whose grasp of God's gift is always partial and hesitating.

Consider, then, first, the great temptation by which the Church is always beset,—to live conformably to the world, and to gain prestige, security and worldly honour. Here is a familiar topic for preachers of the present day, often canvassed, but perhaps nowhere more damagingly than in Emil Brunner's *The Misunderstanding of the Church* (Lutterworth, 1950). This corresponds very well with one force in the pressure brought by the world to bear on Jesus; it is there in the Temptation (Luke 4.1-13); it is there every time they wish 'to make him a king' (e.g. John 6.15). There is always a sense in which the church must take to heart the text, 'Woe to you, when all men speak well of you, for so their fathers did to the false prophets' (Luke 6.26). In the mind of the composer and the performer, then, there must be a vigilant care against the temptation to write and perform in such a way that men shall in this sense 'speak well'; it is this which lies behind that beauty-hunting, that craving for attractiveness, which disfigures so much of the music of the eighteenth and nineteenth centuries.

Allied with this is a temptation to exert influence of a kind not demanded by or exemplified in the Master. There is always a pressure on the church to try to be greater than its Lord. Certain forms of evangelism are tainted with this defect. It means that along with an unregenerate desire for power goes an unwillingness to encounter any tension or difficulty. There is a danger that in the composition and practice of church music the church will always turn to what is easy and familiar, seeking to bring men to Christ by a route which by-passes the way of the Cross. Music which is come by in that frame of mind will not be of profit to the people of God.

But lest any should think that we are beginning to build up a charter for the aesthetic highbrow for whom almost everything that appeals to the ordinary man is common and unclean, let us hasten to say that one of our Lord's major gestures against phari-saism was in the hospitality and 'unshockableness' with which he received into his company all kinds of people for whom society as a whole had no use. He was, we must remember, much too cheerful for the very religious among his enemies, and his disciples were far too sociable (Matt. 11.19; Luke 7.34). Provided it be always borne in mind that the Son of Man was not in fact a glutton and a winebibber, and that whatever company he kept was able to avail itself of his healing and fortifying presence without leaving any stain on him, such texts as those are a salutary reminder that pride and aloofness are no part of the church musician's ministry.

The essence of the Gospel which gives life to the church is in the complete involvement of Christ with the world, together with his moral transcendence of it. The doctrine of the church from which all criticism must proceed has in it a dynamic paradox of 'No' and 'Yes'. The church that was founded in the Incarnation, Passion and Resurrection of Christ is not an institution which invariably says 'Yes' to the world, nor one which invariably says 'No'. It is as fastidious as the man seeking a goodly pearl and as hospitable as the drag-net (Matt. 13.45-7). Therefore if any music be composed or performed with an eye simply to 'attracting' the unconverted, it is liable to fall into the same error that we find in the parson who, in order to make users of bad language feel at home, himself uses bad language and tells doubtful stories. Similarly music written or performed by people who give too much rein to the impulse to select only the most sensitive and best instructed people for disciples, music affectedly forbidding whether in craftsmanship or in choice, will be too much 'on its dignity' to help anybody. There needs to be, in composition and choice, a combination of the 'Yes' and the 'No' that corresponds as exactly as our sinful nature allows to the 'Yes' and 'No' that are in the Word of God.

These are general principles. We can now move one step towards that particularity which is our ultimate goal by observing what has in past ages been the practice of the church.

The most obvious fact to which we can at once point, and which needs little supporting argument, is that in the first stage of music's maturity, the sixteenth century, church music is invariably chamber music. With exceptions too insignificant to give us pause here, all music at that time was chamber-music. It was music designed to be enjoyed by its performers, and, in the case of church music, designed to adorn the liturgy; but it was not primarily music to be listened to by an inactive hearer. When an ordinarily appreciative listener tells me that a whole evening of Tudor madrigals is more of a discipline to him than an entertainment he not only has my personal sympathy, but he is talking good history. The madrigal—secular vocal chamber music of the purest sort—was written for performers, not for listeners; or at any rate not for an indiscriminate audience of the kind for which a modern concert-piece is written.

We need not pause to prove that the church music of the polyphonic school is chamber-music. But what interests us here is that, being so, it is delivered at once from a whole section of temptation—from all the temptation associated with rhetorical techniques. There is in this climate no temptation to undue influence. Nobody is thinking about influence. Except some sacred impresario (such as the Popes for whom Palestrina wrote so much of his music) provide a build-up of publicity, there is nothing in this music of prestige-value. To that extent it is innocent. True, there is that aspect of sixteenth-century polyphonic music which Cecil Forsyth, with characteristic trenchancy, called 'Musical bind-weed' (Stanford and Forsyth, *History of Music*, Macmillan, 1916, pp. 156f.); and there was in medieval music a certain tendency to levity against which ecclesiastical authorities wrote and spoke with a deep frown (for which, if you will, see *The Church and Music*, ch. IV). But it is all innocent in a way in which later music is not innocent, and the complaints of the church, which are summed up in the famous encyclical of Pope John XXII (1325), are normally directed against a lack of clarity, simplicity and decorum which makes the words carried by the music unintelligible to the listener. It is the very reverse of that over-emphasis and rhetorical indulgence which later critics impugn in more highly-developed music.

It is, of course, a sense of this 'innocence' that has caused the reaction of present-day taste in favour of the Tudors. There is a cool impersonal eloquence about the music of this period, from whatever part of Europe it comes, that came as a refreshment to ears too long sated with the over-ripe rhetoric of the Victorians.

Some of this innocence departed after the Restoration in England, and on the Continent with the advent two generations before of homophony. The new convention of the 'accompanied tune', solo prominent and 'accompaniment' in the background, a convention which before 1600 had been limited to the balladry of strolling players, made at once towards rhetorical development. In itself this is not a 'fall'—not an irretrievable step of moral retrogression: it is simply the introduction into music of a new element of risk. But post-Restoration music retains one important element of innocence in that it is written, if not in an age of craftsmanship, at least in an age of hackwork, which is less edifying than craftsmanship but more so than the climate of artist-mysticism which followed it. The texture of eighteenth-century music in England is invariably light, and its style highly conventional. At their best the Restoration composers of England are capable of highly expressive use of the new vocabulary; but in the main the dance-rhythm predominates, and the conventional style provides a fairly strict pattern into which the composer must be humble enough to fit his music. There is room here for inflated bombast of a kind—for reams of really dull music, and we may perhaps say that Purcell's Te Deum in D is one of the earliest examples of empty rhetoric. But even if here or there we find an eighteenth-century musician who could not be described as a hack, the musical ethos of that age was such as to restrain the musician from abrogating to himself too much in the way of rights of self-expression. The same ethos that caused Lord Mornington to be thought a sorry dog for walking through the public street carrying a fiddle-case imposed on music a formality which, while it allowed a good deal of servile dullness of a kind unknown in the polyphonic age, and a certain amount of windy platitude, such as you will find in the worse pages of Boyce's *Cathedral Music*, did at least discourage the more licentious kinds of exhibitionism.

For that reason, eighteenth century music is preferred nowadays, alongside that of the Tudors, to the Victorian idiom. And these preferences are thoroughly healthy. The repertory of our modern cathedrals has been transformed by Fellowes and his disciples, and they deserve our gratitude.

Along with these revivals of older music for the sake of its innocence we must mention the revival of interest in folk song and carols which has been one of the notable features of twentieth-century musical history. Especially in the church we observe such gestures as those by which folk songs have (with astonishing success, despite a few complaints here and there) been adapted for hymns, and carols substituted for the more demonstrative kind of anthem.[1] Here again, we see at work a reaction against the

[1] Familiar examples of folk songs in use as hymn tunes are 'Who would true valour see' (EH 402), 'O God of earth and altar' (EH 562), 'Father, hear the prayer we offer' (EH 385) and 'It is a thing most wonderful' (EH 597). Some comments on the corruption of the carol will be found in my book *The English Carol* (Herbert Jenkins, 1958), chapter 8.

showmanship and portentousness which had all but driven English church music into the ground by 1900, and the content of that reaction is a preference for the innocence of the late medieval folk tune. These things are common knowledge. Where we still lag is in the provision of an explicit principle on which we can distinguish, not only in the music of the past, but in the musical compositions and choices of the present day, what is good from what is pernicious. It is quite clear that music has now lost its innocence. Nobody can now write music innocent in the Tudor way or in the eighteenth-century way. Nobody ought now to insist that the music of innocence or partial innocence is all that our people should hear. That is archaism, which is a refusal to encounter the perils of our age. What we look for is positive doctrinal guidance, and in this chapter I have endeavoured to state its ground. We must now go on to particulars.

CHAPTER EIGHT

METHODS OF CRITICISM

A TYPICAL CONTROVERSY

AT this point I venture on to ground where I would tread warily, and would not seek to offend. But I venture the view, which will have been implicit in what I have written so far, that when our preceptors would defend the necessity of 'raising standards' in our church music, they have yet to find a terminology which is so clearly conformable with the Gospel as decisively to refute the philistines and the slothful.

It will be necessary in this chapter to examine one or two judgments in the Archbishops' Committee's Report, *Music in Church* (SPCK, 1951), and in order to introduce that discussion, I here refer to a somewhat truculent criticism of that report which was made in 1957 by the Bishop of Leicester in a diocesan leaflet. The Bishop contended that the values expressed in the Report were those of 'academic' musicians, and as such irrelevant to the needs of parish churches. His protest was written with the gusto that informs the statements of those who would identify themselves with the 'plain man'. 'We find', he wrote at one point, 'all the usual stress on the necessity of using music properly constructed from the point of view of composition, and all the silly little points of liturgical purism, such as that there must be no recessional hymn after the Blessing, and so on.' The Bishop's article contained also a strenuous plea for 'popular' music in church.

This, of course, provoked great wrath in the leading musicians of the Church of England. The Editor of *English Church Music*, Mr Leonard Blake, in an editorial comment (Vol. 27, no. 3, pp. 65ff.) wrote a strong rejoinder. 'To know that there is a God in heaven,' he said, 'the fountain of all goodness, and not to seek to render to him what is his due is to go the way of eternal damnation. The logical end to the Bishop's argument is to throw up the whole struggle towards better music, decoration, furnishings, or what you will in church, and to let people wallow at whatever levels of taste they were born or have sunk into.' On the Bishop's plea for popular music, Mr Blake wrote, 'We would only suggest that when deep religious conviction is truly popular—natural to the folk, if you like—it will find its own music.'

The tale was taken up by Dr Greenhouse Allt, Principal of Trinity College of Music, in a lecture to the International Association of Organists at their 1957 Conference (reprinted in M. Hinrichsen (ed.), *Organ and Choral Aspects and Prospects*, Hinrichsen, 1958, pp. 49ff.). 'We should tell the Right Reverend the Bishop', said Dr Allt, 'that the cultivated mind of a skilled musician . . . revolts against the use of such a sensuous appeal to replace Church Music, the finest of which is hallowed by tradition, inspired by spiritual experience and capable of satisfying our deepest spiritual needs when there is an understanding and sympathetic mind ready to receive it. Between the kind of emotion stimulated by the crooner, which the Bishop noted drew the young by the thousand, and the emotion stimulated by Church Music for our religious needs, there is a gulf as wide as that between Lazarus in Abraham's bosom and the souls in torment.' His next paragraph makes it clear that Dr Allt has especially been stirred to wrath by the sight of Fr Geoffrey Beaumont's *Folk Mass*, of which more in its place (pp. 104ff).

Now let there be no mistake about your present author's opinion, which is that the document that gave occasion for these denunciations is a repulsive piece of ignorant philistinism evincing an attitude to the musicians of deliberate misunderstanding which is painful enough in the ill-informed, but in the influential, catastrophic. But would that the replies had carried the matter into the Bishop's own ground and been written in theological terms! Responsible and well-informed as they are, you can observe in them at certain points a shying away from the real issue. Mr Blake says that the musicians, if the Bishop is right, may as well throw up the sponge. If the Bishop wished to reply, he would be entitled to say, 'I *am* right. Do that.' When Mr Blake speaks of the 'wallowing' of the ill-informed, the Bishop will have him on the ground of lack of pastoral compassion. When he speaks of religious conviction finding its own music, the Bishop could reply, 'That is what I observed about the *Billy Graham Song Book.*' The saddest part of Dr Allt's retort is his appeal to the fact of church music's being 'hallowed by tradition', which is for several reasons very shaky ground to stand on. If he means that the oldest is the best, he must mean that we have now lost the art, and the Bishop will get in with a point about Father Beaumont. Possibly he begs a question in referring to the spiritual experience that inspired the best church music; that is a matter of personal biography, and cannot fairly be brought in evidence. And when he speaks of the best music satisfying the spiritual needs of the sympathetic mind, why should not the Bishop and his friends say, 'We are not sympathetic minds. We do not accept any of this. Do we then not go to heaven?'

I mention that small controversy largely because it is topical, and because it turns on the Archbishops' Committee's Report. It is not in itself of enormous importance, but it does fairly indicate along what lines the musicians defend themselves in these times. Their defence, though nobly intentioned, is quite disastrously insecure.

THE ARCHBISHOPS' COMMITTEE'S REPORT

Now what did the Report say about the general principles of judgment? It is in all manner of ways an admirable document, and indeed I do not know how an official document could have been better prepared. But I take the key-sentence to be the following, from page 7:

> Music that is in keeping with the spirit of the liturgy will be characterized by qualities of nobility and restraint; by freedom

from sensationalism or mawkishness, and from all suggestions of secularity.

That expresses very well the general view of the best church musicians to-day. I believe its authors pondered it long, and compared it with the corresponding passage in the 1922 Report, before committing themselves to it. But at three points a hostile critic would, I believe, ask for explanation.

The first is in the word 'nobility'. Louis Bouyer, in his remarkable book, *Life and Liturgy* (Sheed & Ward, 1956), writes in his opening pages of a romantic corruption of the liturgical spirit which had the consequence that 'the most obvious features of (the liturgy) were those embodying the external pomp, decorum and grandeur befitting so majestic a Prince' (p. 4). Later in the same book he writes of the special problems presented by the psychological self-consciousness of modern men to those who would follow the way of mysticism, and the great dangers which the temptation to 'self-centred mysticism' presents in these days (pp. 252f.). Is it altogether unfair to claim to overhear in a word like 'nobility' an echo of self-conscious romantic mysticism? The great liturgists avoid this kind of speech to such purpose that it is possible for Romano Guardini to write in his book, *The Spirit of the Liturgy* (Sheed & Ward, 1937) of 'the playfulness of the liturgy'.

Secondly, 'sensationalism and mawkishness' are words of doubtful value. They are words of moral tone, and therefore need some explanatory conjunction with the aesthetic field in which the whole Report is necessarily written. It should have been possible, says the hostile critic, to find words of clearer meaning which presupposed less sympathy in the reader.

Thirdly, the condemnation of the secular makes us ask at once, What about the carols? The precept is one of decent prudence: it would be an unwise organist who offered the latest 'hot' number as an outgoing voluntary (and that opinion will be reviewed in a moment); and many feel that the *Londonderry Air* is an unsuitable vehicle even for the highly emotional hymns to which it is usually set. But still—were the Thaxted churchwardens right after all in protesting against the display in their parish church of the carol, 'Tomorrow shall be my dancing day'?

I believe that the best word of criticism that the Report offers in a general way is on p. 39, where, dealing with hymn tunes, it is written:

> It is because the tunes of songs have the power to conjure an image and an ideal that it is necessary to be sure that the music of hymns does not insinuate a conception of Christ markedly weaker and more limited than the picture of the Incarnate Son of God revealed in the Bible.

That is admirably said; we could have welcomed more of that. But on the whole the tone of the Report is vaguely Levitical:

> The rhythm should have life and movement without levity, and dignity without heaviness. The melody of all the parts, not of the treble only, should be shapely in outline, and neither angular nor dull; in general it should be diatonic, and chromatic intervals should be only sparingly used. The harmony should be for the most part simple, avoiding excessive use of discords which introduce a note of vulgarity or triviality, and which pall with repetition (p. 6).

That is all very well as part of a manual of instructions for students learning to write hymn tunes; but it is, as a canon of 'Church Music, suitable and unsuitable', distressingly imprecise. What we gather from the Report, indeed, is that while its authors are quite clear about their Christian convictions, and skilful in diagnosing current diseases, they are far from clear about the connection between the moral principles and the diagnoses. The consequence is that now and again they produce very doubtful judgments in particular cases. After all, if angularity in melody is reprehensible, must we dismiss the hymn tune *St Mary* (EH 84)? If chromatic harmony is dangerous, what becomes of a good deal of J. S. Bach? And when the authors are betrayed into holding up as examples of good writing in hymn tunes such ponderous effusions as Stanford's *Engelberg* (AM 527) and Harwood's *Thornbury* (AM 256) we are really brought up short. They, and for all I know, my reader,

E

may not agree that those tunes are to be so described; but on what grounds, in the Report, are they found defensible?

A BOOK BY DR MARTIN SHAW

Another document, this time strictly pedagogic, which has had much influence and a very large proportion of which is first rate material, is Dr Martin Shaw's *The Principles of Church Music Composition* (1921). This is not only a book whose principles are entirely accepted by the most discerning musicians of today, but also a singularly interesting piece of methodology for our purposes here. His opening point is that the 'rules of harmony' prescribed in Sir John Stainer's *Primer of Harmony* (in those days, but not in these, a familiar textbook) are demonstrably legalistic and at certain points misleading; he shows that in the Tudor composers there are frequent 'breaches' of Stainer's 'rules'— those of 'consecutive fifths' and of 'false relations'. The matter is now only of historic interest, but we give it this passing attention because what Dr Shaw ought to have said, surely, was that Stainer's 'rules', or more properly 'abstractions' are bye-laws which are, in the vocabulary with which Stainer was concerned, binding. Dr Shaw is so clear that that vocabulary has been exhausted that he does not think the point worth making; but his omission of it is an indication of an anterior bias which affects his subsequent judgments. And indeed the point can be nicely illustrated by asking any unprejudiced observer whether Dr Shaw's harmonization of that tedious but typically post-baroque melody, *The First Nowell* (Oxford Book of Carols, 27) is really more 'in character' than the familiar version of Stainer which most people still know and use.[1]

Dr Shaw then proceeds to state a number of precepts concerning church music composition, some of which are obvious, some illuminating, some dubious. He says, for example, that monotone

[1] First printed in Bramley & Stainer, *Christmas Carols New and Old* (1871); hymn book editions almost always alter it for the worse, but in popular use Stainer is nearly invariable.

in the melody of a hymn tune is undesirable. He gives several examples, including the famous and much maligned tune by Dykes to 'Christian dost thou see them'. (AM 91). But nowhere does he give a hint of the reasons why this precept may now and again be effectively set aside. Had he explained why his own tune *Herald* (EH 205) sets it aside he would certainly have had to admit Dykes, who is aiming in his tune at the same menacing or ominous effect that Dr Shaw is seeking in his own. Again, Dr Shaw, among much that is useful and right, says that 'sequence' in a melody is normally weak. Sequence is the repetition of a short phrase a tone or semitone higher or lower—in this fashion.

EH 375

That is a purely temperamental judgment. It is unpractical academicism of the worst kind to call 'weak' such tunes as *Carlisle* (EH 236), *Richmond* (EH 375), *Bishopthorpe* (EH 408) and *Surrey* (EH 491) on the ground of sequential melody. Sir Sydney Nicholson, writing on Improvisation in *A Manual of English Church Music* (SPCK, 1923, pp. 85ff.) positively encourages sequence as a device of musical argument. Had Dr Shaw said that to make a sequence the *prevailing idea* of a melody is a confession of weakness, he would have had the right of it. It is surely clear that a line like this:

Cong. Hymnary 199

is, as an opening line, 'weak' in a sense in which most tunes which have sequence in their penultimate lines are not.

'SCHIZOPHRENIA'

There is no need to pursue this controversy. What matters is that so much precept from the musicians is in this fashion shaky and contradictory. Indeed, when we hear much of what is said in lectures and written in books by musicians on these matters of casuistry and morals, we find in them something corresponding to the preacher's disease of 'schizophrenia' which is so ably exposed by R. E. C. Browne in his recent book, *The Ministry of the Word* (SCM, *Studies in Ministry & Worship*, 1957). I do not know that the present condition of church music moralism could be better described than in Mr Browne's words about the preacher:

> A schizophrenic is not a Jekyll and Hyde personality but a personality so split into isolated fragments that coherent speech and action have died in the death of any single purpose which could be the integrating force of the personality. . . . The term 'schizophrenia' will be used here to indicate the condition of a minister of the Word who holds two contradictory sets of doctrines at the same time, one set being unconsciously held and showing itself through the unspoken assumptions which inform parts of his utterances and make for inconsistencies in his pastoral and evangelistic policy. . . .
>
> The 'schizophrenic' is the man who tidies up his mind and keeps it tidy: in speech he will tend to be boisterously dogmatic, in the wrong sense of being dogmatic, or he will avoid matters of importance, restricting himself to questions of marginal concern . . . 'Schizophrenia' is avoided by forswearing all false simplifications so as to maintain the essential untidiness of mind consequent on the acceptance of Christian doctrine. This essential untidiness is preserved by habitual refusal to come to definite conclusions where there can be none, without ever denying the value of either thought so limited or the forms of speech which embody such a doctrinal position (pp. 42, 49).

Boisterous dogmatism is a very fair description of Dr Martin Shaw's paper, and of a good deal else purveyed by musicians in the field of morals. Too much 'tidiness' in the condemnation of this and the approval of that has led to such contradictions as we have already referred to, in consequence of a divorce between the over-hasty practical precept and the imperfectly formulated doctrine from which it proceeds.

If there is one point of dogmatism that is especially in danger of damaging the true form of church music today, it may well be this insistence on 'nobility' and 'dignity', and I believe that it is a mistake to regard these as inseparable properties of Christian worship—even of English Christian worship. But it would be mere legalism to outlaw them altogether. The clue is St Thomas's *proportio sive consonantia*. At a Coronation the occasion requires dignity, and the music prepared for the 1953 Coronation was notable not least for the exceedingly skilful way in which its compilers expressed the counterpoint of dignities that formed the texture of that service. Parry's 'I was glad' and Walton's Te Deum between them sum it up: the Westminster scholars are once in their lifetimes permitted to shout in church. And the glory of the Te Deum is expressed in a piece of rhythmic vitality that suggests all heaven dancing: but there were other moods, adequately met by a pageant of composers from Gibbons to Howells.

The mistake is to equate all worship too closely with the most august occasions. The august is, precisely, 'occasional'. The every-day needs to be lighter, more down-to-earth. The humanly pompous is permissible only when the general context is the Incarnation. That, after all, was 'down to earth'.

CHAPTER NINE

BAD MUSIC

A BAD HYMN TUNE

If the Old Testament urges us to avoid pride, and the New
Testament to look for positive good; if the doctrine of the church
which we hold insists that our behaviour, and therefore our church
music, be conformable to the Gospel which is in the life, passion
and resurrection of Christ, what should we say about the prevalent
abuses in church music?

We may begin with one or two examples of music which is
widely held to be inferior, and which we agree to be inferior.
Take first this highly conventional hymn tune

EH Appendix 36

That is probably a tune that today has few friends. On the other hand, the only charge that can be brought against it under the categories ordinarily in use is that it is quite wonderfully dull. Perhaps the most damaging of the 'foreground' criticisms that we should want to make of it is that it entirely lacks, and lacked at the time of its composition, any element of 'newness', that it offends in not displaying that freshness, that *nitor*, which the Scholastics demanded of good art. That is indeed true. In another place (*The Music of Christian Hymnody*, pp. 270f.) I have collected a by no means exhaustive assembly of hymn tunes of this period that begin with that particular three-note pattern. What is 'new' must be i n controversy with what is 'old', and the real vice that lies behind this kind of composition is a fear of that controversy, a fear of 'newness'. That fear will always result in the replacement of *nitor*, of freshness and affirmation, by a kind of dull negation. The 'newness' which (see above, p. 34) J. E. Barton required of good art corresponds with the 'newness' in the biblical expression 'Behold, I make all things new' (Rev. 21.5) or in 'a new creation' (II Cor. 5.17). Church music should manifest this 'newness', and that hymn tune, like so many, fails to do so. It is important to note that at the time of its composition it failed here; it is not that it has been obscured by a large number of imitations. This kind of 'newness' does not, as a matter of fact, tarnish in this way; imitations never obscure it. In the beginning its composer was too ready to accept what he had been given in the way of conventional music and conventional religion. He said 'Yes' too often: and the result was a 'No' in his music. Much of this kind of music is world-denying and in the end faith-denying because it relies too much on security.

71

SANKEY AND GRAHAM

I believe that this is the main charge that is to be brought against the hymnody of popular evangelism. It should be noted at once that to associate the worst excesses of evangelical hymnody with the name of Ira D. Sankey is to do Sankey injustice. A careful study of *Sacred Songs and Solos* reveals Sankey as by far the best composer of sacred choruses who has ever attempted the technique. Although he wrote too much, he was capable of an originality and variety of styles which his imitators could not compass. They were not disposed to try. Of that whole school, only Sankey, who had a real first-hand contact with the folk music of his time, and could achieve in words and music a light touch, could have written this merry masterpiece:

6   Sacred Songs & Solos, 432

At the feast of Bel-shaz-zar and a thou - sand of his lords, while they drank from gol - den ves-sels as the Book of Truth re-cords: In the night as they re-vell'd in the roy - al pal - ace hall they were seiz'd with con - ster na-tion 'twas the Hand up - on the wall!

But the imitators of Sankey tended all to write in one style, one of their chief musical obsessions being a rising sixth in a plagal-mode tune, of this sort:

That phrase appears hundreds of times in *Sacred Songs and Solos*, and could be called the 'signature' of that kind of evangelical composer. The principle here, as it was with the more conventional tune, is that it is all too complacent to be conformable with the Gospel. There is no tension in it; all is repose. As an agent of the Gospel it is absolutely misleading. One may judge that in the original Sankey movement there was so much improvisation and hasty composition that inevitably a large number of tunes and hymns appeared on a standard pattern. But we cannot denounce too strongly the premeditated and professional use of music of this kind for the purposes of evangelism. We have already remarked on the curious fact that zeal for souls goes with debased musical taste. We now feel able to assert that the debased musical taste, and especially the deliberate debasement of musical taste, tells us something sinister about the evangelism. For although in themselves the 'Sankey' tunes were originally designed to bring a sense of security to people who had physically as well as spiritually lost it, their present-day use can only have the effect of saying to men and women 'Peace, peace' where there is no peace. The contents of the *Billy Graham Song Book* may be conformable to the Gospel as preached by that evangelist. They are not conformable to the Gospel as it stands in Scripture. There is in them not only no 'newness' but a positive denial of 'newness'; the modern examples were deliberately contrived in order to express a 'Yes' to the standards of the world which denies the Gospel's 'No'. That is why they intentionally exploit the musical platitude, the cliché of rhythm and phrase. In their modern form they express a power-mysticism, a bid for 'influence' over a partly drugged mob, which is an open defiance of the example of Christ. Their 'heartiness' is a resurrection without passion: factitious sentiment generated by quickly-resolved discords in the harmony is substituted for Passion.

This criticism can be linked with what was said on an earlier page if we will consider how far what is sometimes represented as a response to evangelism is tainted with spiritual cupidity. It could probably be said that in so far as that taint is there, the art associated with that evangelism will be corrupted. The ugliness of 'evangelical' music is of a piece not only with the flashy ugliness of the décor that often goes with it in its modern forms, but with the pretentious ugliness of the worst of the Victorian chapels. Its progenitor in the end is greed.

IMMODESTY

'Newness' in the fullest sense is always difficult to command, and its absence is too easily accepted. The best way to prepare for it is the ascetic way. Greed kills it. But in church, of all places, it should be looked for. We may proceed to consider one or two pieces of music which are widely approved but upon which we would throw doubt.

The new cult of congregational singing has brought many blessings: but it brings also in the musicians certain delusions of grandeur. Especially is this true when musicians write hymn tunes particularly designed for very large gatherings. The organizers of hymn festivals and such activities should beware of this. The danger here is to produce what is broadly rhetorical but what is intellectually and in the end spiritually defective. Perhaps the Wesleys and their followers were the first to be thus tempted. The enormous popularity of hymn singing which was the result of their work produced in hymnody a debased coinage such as we see, especially, in the post-Methodist hymnody of the early nineteenth century. The symptoms of intellectual decay are always to be seen in the bass of any monodic tune. (And by the bass I mean the bass naturally demanded by the tune, not a more 'interesting' but adventitious bass added by an ingenious improver.) This is the bass line of a very celebrated Methodist tune of about 1800: after contemplating it for a minute, the reader will need no further argument.

Methodist Hymn Book 371(i)

But in more recent times the cult of the 'big tune' has extended itself to non-enthusiastic congregations, with results which sometimes excel in dignity and pomposity but are woefully short of significance. These are charges which I believe could be brought against many of the hymn tunes of W. H. Ferguson, as well as against *Thornbury* (AM 256) and *Engelberg* (AM 527) which we mentioned above. There is in those tunes a lack of melodic decisiveness which is apparently compensated by a richness of harmonic texture, and the cause of the trouble was a tendency to think in too large terms of the purpose which a hymn tune should fulfil. They lack that essential modesty which is the primary virtue in a hymn tune. The modern grandiose style originated in the large post-Arnold public-school congregation, and its use tends to generate a soft-hearted bonhomie which is religiously unedifying.

THE BETTER WAY

But it is better that we become clear about the virtue of the good than that we spend much time denouncing the inferior. It is clear, surely, that what have come to be acknowledged our great hymn tunes, 'hallowed by tradition' if you will, have in them a 'newness', together with a modesty of bearing, that has, to put it crudely and practically, made them last. 'Newness' was easily to be achieved when not many tunes were being written, and modesty was easily achieved by men of the puritan persuasion: that explains the magnificent sufficiency of the puritan psalm-tunes of Geneva and England. The 'modesty' of the primitive Lutheran chorale (which J. S. Bach entirely overshadowed in his magnificent, but out of context grandiose, arrangements) is seen in its innocent rhythmic drive and enthusiasm.

Despite the debasement of the coinage through inflation, first as the consequence of the Methodist Revival and later as the consequence of the new ease of music-printing, a steady stream of 'new' and 'modest' hymnody can be discerned throughout the generations that follow the Puritan inception of hymnody. And although the spate of publications increases so calamitously, the stream itself does not appreciably lessen in breadth or volume. There are as many first-rate eighteenth-century hymn tunes and nineteenth-century hymn tunes as there are of the sixteenth century; the good coin is not here, as by Gresham's law, driven out by the bad. It is only that the temptation to write at all, and the temptation to write badly, are so much more clamorous in the later age of easy communication.[1] But there is no case for saying that, say, the Psalm tune *Winchester Old* (1592), which we sing to 'While shepherds watched' is a better tune than *David's Harp* (1701: EH 378), or *University* (1789: EH 93), or Steggall's *Christchurch* (1865: EH 411), or Vaughan Williams's *Down Ampney*

[1] Refer again to the footnote on p. 32.

(1906: EH 152), all of which are typically 'children of their age'.

It might be worth pointing out here that, in the matter of new hymnody, insufficient notice has been taken of the very remarkable gestures towards both newness and modesty that were published in that theologically eccentric hymn book, *Songs of Praise*. Some of the more conventional of the new material in that book was incorporated in the 1933 edition of the *English Hymnal*, but the composer who has most suffered from public neglect in that book was Gustav Holst. More than any other, he has pointed the way to a new clarity of line and taut reticence of rhetoric which has been followed by no other English composer, but which suggests much more some of the latest examples of Continental reformed hymnody to be found, for example, in the *Gesangbuch* (1953) of the Swiss Reformed Church. There is no doubt at all that the group of musicians of whom Holst was a distinguished member were greatly impressed by the over-demonstrativeness and lack of modesty in what had gone just before: and Holst more even than Vaughan Williams exploited the possibilities of pure counterpoint in his writing, just as he did in his secular works, with results of which more note should nowadays be taken.

The other developments of any significance can, I believe, be found in the *BBC Hymn Book*. While that book is not free from examples of an inflated 'Public School' style, here and there, and especially in the work of Professor W. K. Stanton, we find an urge towards contrapuntal controversy within the texture of a tune which bespeak a real awareness of the controversy of the Gospel. His best example of this is in the last two phrases of *Hambleden* (314 i)—a tune whose large scale rhetoric is uniquely matched by internal intellectual integrity. His *Sherston* (287 i) was an earlier gesture in the same direction, and its ferocious modulation, while perhaps too dramatic to attain even that success which a good tune should be allowed, is at any rate a piece of pure courage. Another fine example of that diatonic counterpoint which always best expresses the controversy of reality is towards the end of Herbert Murrill's *Carolyn* (273 i).

When we turn away from hymns—which must always occupy most of our time, because they are in English churches so peculiarly the people's music—to consider church music in larger forms, the same pattern is to be found. Having already made some observations on the earlier styles, I here confine my observations to this: that although the Victorian age was as prodigal of second-hand, complacent anthems exploiting superficial dramatic effects and making religion altogether too familiar and obvious to be true, as it was of illusively restful hymn tunes (such as *Crimond* and 'Abide with me'), the generation in which we now stand is very far from immune from temptations to prodigality. Indeed, while the publication of new hymn tunes is a much more difficult matter than it formerly was, because of the standardization of hymnody within denominations and the relatively small flow of hymn books compared with the dozens that were put out within any decade between 1850 and 1900, the publication of new anthems seems to be still regarded as a prosperous proposition. With one or two notable and admirable exceptions, the anthems now coming from the Presses are alarmingly complacent in their short-skirted modern fashion. Not now the thunders of Steggall's 'God came from Teman' or the drawing-room urbanities of Goss and Stainer —which produced, as we readily grant, a vertiginous progress from the ridiculous to the blasphemous and back; but we have a new technique of deprecating platitude which is best to be observed in the multitude of hymn-anthems that are replacing those older, and devotionally sturdier, settings of Scripture. It is accepted now that a familiar hymn tune decorated from verse to verse with a more or less stereotyped pattern of organistic and choral adornment, will do very well for an anthem. If the composer is feeling on good form, he may write the hymn tune himself. But beyond these, we have multitudes of settings of biblical or non-biblical words written down to the capacities of small choirs, whose smoothness and attractiveness are, when taken in a considerable series, hardly less delusive than the 'rest' cult of Sankey. There is far more downright complacency in modern anthem writing than in modern hymn tune writing. Modest music carved out of hard material is difficult, at the time of writing, to come by, but we can expect it from Mr John Joubert, Dr Armstrong Gibbs, Dr Geoffrey Bush, Professor Hutchings and Professor Herbert Howells.[1]

English church music has seldom, indeed, been better served at any period than it has been by the settings of the Evening Canticles written recently by Herbert Howells. Of these the most famous, and perhaps in all ways the best, is the *Collegium Regale*, composed for King's College, Cambridge.[2] This setting displays what is to be found in the settings also for Worcester (A minor), Westminster Abbey (B minor) and St Paul's Cathedral (G minor) —a profound sense of the mystery of the Incarnation before which the musician becomes, at the beginning, almost inarticulate, but which brings him in the end to abundant joy in the *Gloria*.

[1] A word may be added here about three books of anthems which have come into use during the past two decades. *The Church Anthem Book* (ed. Walford Davies and Henry Ley, Oxford University Press, 1933) is a collection of 100 anthems, surveying the whole field of church music and making what turns out to be a very judicious selection. There is little complacency in it, but complaints are sometimes heard of the difficulty of some of the pieces. Their chief difficulty is not for the singers but, in the accompanied anthems, for the organist, who is often called on to make an organ arrangement of a two-stave pianistic accompaniment. In such numbers as 'Jesu, Joy of man's desiring' and Brahms's 'We love the place' an organ accompaniment ought to have been provided. But apart from this there is no doubt that this is the best one-volume collection available.

The Oxford Easy Anthem Book (Oxford University Press, 1956) contains 50 anthems most of which, as the title implies, are well within the capacity of the ordinary four-part choir. Again there is a good selection from all periods, and the chief pitfalls are to be found in certain modern works which are not above the platitude and the restatement of the obvious.

The Novello Anthem Book (Novello, no date, but recent) has the great disadvantage of being compiled entirely from recent publications of Novello; there is one anthem (of 50) by Schutz and one by Schicht (early 19th century), and two by Bach; Parry, Stanford and G. C. Martin alone stand between these and the modern period. This selection needs to be used with great care if, as a choir's normal musical diet, it is not to produce week by week a pageant of contemporary truisms.

[2] Recorded 78 r.p.m. Columbia LX1572.

Stanford's great series of settings, from the B flat (1879)[1] to the C major (1909) contain more fine music than any that had been written for three centuries before him; they are rich and expansive, and varied in their treatment of the words. But even the G major, that tour-de-force for treble solo and full choir with organ, is not exempt from the generalization that these services begin and end with a sound, healthy Victorian confidence. One has only to compare Stanford's openings with those of Howells;

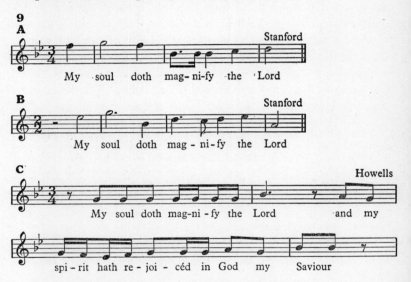

to see how far Howells has advanced towards a new expression of humility-without-sadness which is as good an example as will be found anywhere at the moment of the genuine service of the Faith by music.

There is in the recent music of this composer not only for choir but also for that more intractable instrument, the organ, a clarity of line and an essential reticence and control within the rich fabric of sound which are an example to all who would write for the church. The six organ pieces published in 1951 by Novello,

[1] Recorded 78 r.p.m. Columbia LX1388.

including the *Sarabande for the Morning of Easter*, though not
overtly designed as an expression of public religious experience,
are easily the most essentially Christian music offered by any
contemporary English composer for that instrument, and are
almost alone worthy to stand alongside the music that is coming
from contemporary composers on the Continent for their combination of inner integrity and foreground relevance.

It is, in this sphere, only possible to say 'what kind of thing
happens' when music is at its best in church. Moreover, it would
be indelicate to particularize what we believe to be the defects of
recently published compositions. But we may turn now to the
practical aspects of the church musician's work, and apply the
categories to them which have here been tentatively applied to
compositions.

A NOTE ON STAINER'S *THE CRUCIFIXION*

After the completion of the first draft of this book I was urged
by a reader to add this note on the most famous—perhaps the
most notorious—of all Passiontide cantatas. I do it with a certain
unwillingness. I had intended not to mention this work, partly
because the criticisms against it are by now familiar enough, and
partly because those who love it are usually too greatly offended by
the very act of criticism to be able to attend to the criticism's
content.

E. H. Fellowes, in *English Cathedral Music* (Methuen, 1941,
p. 223), said in a few words all that need be said about the music
of this work. 'It suffers', he wrote, 'primarily from the extreme
poverty, not to say triviality, of the musical ideas dealing with a
subject which should make the highest demand for dignity of
treatment.' It is, he further said, 'a work for which no musician
can honestly find a word of praise.'

It is difficult to add much to that, except that here and there we
seem to see not so much a poor musical idea as a failure, to develop
it, or to build it into a coherent architectural scheme. It could be

said, for example, that the 'Procession to Calvary' (Novello, vocal score, no. 3) begins with a quite impressive musical idea; but it must be admitted that the middle section of that chorus, at the words 'Though weary and worn', is a sorry contrast. The best music in the whole work is in the final hymn-tune; and the musical secret is perhaps that Stainer, like so many of his contemporaries, was defective in the constructional faculty that is indispensable for the composition of a coherent and consistent piece of music more than sixteen bars long.

I am personally convinced, however, that it is the libretto that kills the work. 'Stainer', says Fellowes, 'was particularly unfortunate in his librettist.' Indeed he was. Here is a sample:

> So thou liftest Thy divine petition
>   Pierced with cruel anguish through and through;
> So thou grievest o'er our lost condition,
>   Pleading, 'Ah, they know not what they do.'
> Oh! 'twas love, in love's divinest feature,
>   Passing o'er that dark and murd'rous blot,
> Finding e'en for each low fallen creature,
>   Tho' they slay thee, one redeeming spot.
> Yes! and still Thy patient Heart is yearning
>   With a love that mortal scarce can bear,
> Thou in pity, deep, divine and burning
>   Liftest e'en for me Thy mighty prayer.
> So Thou pleadest e'en for my transgression,
>   Bidding me look up, and trust, and live;
> So thou murmurest Thine intercession,
>   Yea, he knew not; for My sake, forgive.

Confronted with a libretto like that, one wonders how Stainer could resist setting it as he did, to music of which the following are examples.

We have here, in fact, pietism at its unhappiest, a preoccupation with individual sin, an almost morbid gloating over individual badness, together with a resigned and, at times almost a querulous

14

14a

Saviour (compare the emphasis in Chorus 18 on the words 'Is it nothing to you?'). The religious texture of the words is so theologically repulsive that it would have taken a Bach (as we have seen above) to make anything of it; and even Bach might have sent it back for revision.

I wrote an extended criticism of this work, along these lines, in the *British Weekly* for 30 May 1957. I ask leave to quote here from the correspondence my article provoked.

'We were reminded that the late E. H. Fellowes described the music as utter rubbish. I wonder if he had done better himself? For that part, I wonder what E.R. has done to enrich our church musical repertoire. Does he content himself in the capacity of critic par excellence?

'The Crucifixion will continue to be liked by both choir masters and a sympathetic listening public.'

'It is significant that *Crucifixion* is sneered at by those whose choirs and congregations have a capacity for either the purity and high quality of Bach or the intricacies and tonalities of contemporary composers. . . . Such critics can well afford to sneer in high disdain.'

These passages I dare to quote only because I am sure that their authors will not be caused to think again by anything that is written here. What matters is that *The Crucifixion* (and to a less extent Maunder's *Olivet to Calvary*, which is less unfortunate in its words and more so in its music) has engaged the irrational sympathies of a very large section of the Christian public, and is by them all placed beyond criticism. This irrational engagement is a very pure example of the worst crime that an artist (or an evangelist) can commit. I feel, then, that it is fair to say (*a*) that the music of this work is second-rate; (*b*) that its libretto is profane and unpleasant beyond what a church should tolerate, and (*c*) that the worst thing about it is what it has done to people.

CHAPTER TEN

PRACTICAL MATTERS

MUSIC in the service of the church is not at its best when it is trying to be master; but neither is it at its best when it is a slave. God's design for the whole hierarchy of his creation is that that which serves shall serve freely, and that which receives service shall receive it with reverence. The kind of advice which ought to be given to church musicians—among whom I here include not only composers and performers, but also those whose responsibility it is to direct and choose music for the church—should not fall short of that elementary theological requisite. There is no reason at all for repressiveness in the attitude of the church towards musicians, or in that of highly-placed musicians towards their juniors. There is no reason why musicians should be made to feel that they must abandon all sense of vocation or style or even perfection when they serve the church. The church may ask for service, but it should not think itself profitably served by a deaf and dumb handmaid. If it does, the result will be a failure in *proportio sive consonantia* in its music. Let us then apply some of our principles to the various modes in which music serves the church.

THE ORGANIST AND HIS INSTRUMENT

The organist has at his command, as the authors of the Archbishops' Committee's Report of 1922 (*Music in Worship*) wisely warned him, an instrument of 'greater depth, power, range and variety of tone than any other'. Even a small organ is an instrument of considerable power in relation to the building in which it stands, unless (as in Kelham Chapel) it is deliberately voiced very quietly.

The organist should at the outset reckon with the temptations that go with this fact. No musician is faced with so complete a paradigm of the temptation of being shown 'all the kingdoms of the world'. None is from the very beginning placed in a position of such potential power over others as is he. Your virtuoso pianist is restrained by the ascetic discipline required of him to bring him to concert standard. The most eminent of conductors is restrained by the necessity of establishing an intimate and vital relation with the members of his orchestra. But your organist, without making any effort at all, without any practice, without the possibility of being prevented by anything but an upsurge of popular opinion, can make more physical noise, and can exercise more affective power over other people than anybody.

Therefore, more than with any other instrument, the musician who would handle the organ is obliged to see the whole of his discipline along the line of asceticism. The very nature of his instrument is *prima facie* against him if he would produce a musically good and religiously edifying performance on it; he must restrain all the time impulses which the instrument itself and its position 'over against' the congregation raise in him to exercise power.

This is why, as I have heard a distinguished minister who is also a musician tell a body of organists, nothing 'gives you away' so completely as the way in which you play the organ. Aside from the acknowledged virtuosi, to hear a series of amateur organists accompanying a service—especially playing hymns, where their exercise of power is demanded in full measure—is to look at a case-history of nervous and psychological maladjustments. This is said not in disparagement of amateur organists—without whom, a large and benevolent fraternity, our church music would be impossible to sustain at all. It is simply to say that your professional organist may well have been trained to dissemble where your amateur has not been apprised of any such necessity. It is fair to add that the conduct of some professionals on the organ is as 'buttoned-up' and non-committal as you would expect of a man who knew how he would give himself away if he allowed himself to act with any freedom.

The psychology of organ-playing is a study of which psychiatrists have taken too little advantage. Very broadly, evidences of maladjustment are usually to be found in over-use of reed tone, and over-use of deep 16-foot pedal tone. The reasons are not at all recondite. Reed tone is the most dramatic of the tone-colours that the organ can produce; it represents the trumpets which have always been the most evocative of all instruments. It is there to be used, but used sparingly. The deep pedal tone, which most people regard as the *differentia* of the organ, has a double significance— that of security in a general psychological way, and also the practical usefulness of drawing a decent veil over the slothful vagaries of the left hand. Therefore every good organ teacher tells his pupil to be sparing of splashy reed effects, and trains his pupil on Bach trios with an uncompromising eight-foot pedal.

The compulsion towards power is diversified in various fugitive devices for obtaining cheap effect. The temptation on the organist is always to attempt effect at the expense of accuracy, to play such pieces as will produce impressiveness with the least effort,—to play the *Toccata in D minor* of Bach without its Fugue. In order to cover up a tendency to be short of left-hand discipline, he is tempted to add sub-foundational tones to his manual registration. And it is not altogether to be counted merely his misfortune that many present-day church organs (built twenty or more years ago) are so designed tonally as to minister to these temptations, because it was usually he that prescribed their design.

What is known as the 'baroque' movement in organ-craft has in our own time rendered the signal service of uncovering at once a whole complex of unsuspected psychological states in our organists. That movement, if we may so compendiously refer to it, has been a reaction against characteristic 'muddiness' in organ voicing and playing towards clarity. The organ in the Royal Festival Hall is the instrument around which controversy has chiefly gathered. Symbolically, its designers made no attempt to conventionalize even the arrangement of its pipes; and many who heard it were at first shocked at its lack of what has been called for many generations 'typical organ tone'. But 'typical organ tone' of the kind not provided at the Festival Hall is not so much tone as atmosphere—expressible in such romantic words as 'roll', or 'thunder'. What happens at the Festival Hall, or in other places where organs of that tonal texture have been erected (nowhere more effectively than in the small chapel of University College, Oxford)[1] is that the listener hears precisely what is played, not a translation of what is played through a building of high resonance and registration of complex and inharmonious voices.

It is here my contention that, at this time where we now stand, the movement towards clarity and away from 'atmosphere' is entirely right and for the Christian edifying. It makes for honesty. It also—and this is not secondary to but collateral with the other proposition—makes for practical usefulness. For what we said above about the tendency of organists to over-use reeds and heavy deep tones is not entirely the fault of the players. Their organs, liberally supplied with fat foundational diapasons, are as inept for accompanying congregations or choirs as they could be. It is well known to organists, and it will be obvious to anybody else, that when a congregation looks for 'support' from the organ, it looks for what it can hear, but not for what will drown it or oppress it; and that a quite mild tone that includes a reasonable proportion of upper partials is just as effective as a heavy tone including mostly foundationals, and far more restful and conducive to good rhythmical singing. But if his organ provides for such effects only in the reed department, with perhaps a doubtful 'mixture' or two, how can the organist be blamed for not resisting the temptation to pile on the reeds in order to give the congregation 'something to walk on'? Similarly, the pedal departments of most English organs are designed not to give a clear bass-line to the music, but to give

---

[1] In the Appendix (p. 111) the specification of this 'ideal small organ' is reproduced, by kind permission of the organist, Mr John Webster, and the authorities at University College.

a heavy bass-line, and the wearisome continuance of 16-foot diapason tone is the organist's only alternative to the complete absence of 16-foot tone: which last he hesitates to use because he is then playing at the same pitch at which the congregation is singing, and is consequently inaudible.

Life is, of course, made the more interesting and difficult for the organist by the fact that he must be at various points in his work arranger, extemporizer and even composer as well as player. In extemporization he is liable to horrific displays of intemperance, and to correct this his musical vocabulary should be extensive and available on call; he should be readier to extemporize in three parts than in five or six, and should take care by correct timing of his voluntaries to see that his gift is not called into action so frequently as to debase its quality. He must often play from piano-scores, not infrequently from piano reductions of orchestral scores, and he must translate these into organ-language, deciding where the pedal must take the bass line, and where a part must be brought out as a solo. And in the playing of congregational hymns he has to reckon with the fact (it undoubtedly is a fact, and not a fancy) that the four-part vocal score of a hymn tune is not necessarily to be followed with fundamentalist fidelity, but that (*a*) where the people are singing in harmony, inversion of parts to form a decent organ descant is not merely permissible but in a long hymn desirable, and (*b*) where a special unison effect is called for, the whole tune, harmony and all, calls often for rearrangement (but see below, p. 98).

All these duties fall to him, and all need to be performed with such personal restraint that those whom he is serving will notice the music only as a discreet underlining of the sentiments they are themselves directing to the end of worship. Most of the work of the best organists is directly observable only to the critical ears of fellow-organists. But if organists can be taught that to be too spiritually-minded to play the right notes, to prefer impressiveness to accuracy, to bully the congregation, to be glumly reticent and kill the music stone dead by a sulky insensitiveness, are all traceable in the end to sins of the flesh, and curable by the making good of gaps in belief and doctrine, we shall see both amateur and professional looking on their work with new eyes. At least it can now be said, that, if they will accept it, the organ builders are helping them.

PIPES OR ELECTRONES?

A word may be expected here on the vexatious question whether the electronic organ is an adequate substitute for a pipe organ in places whose financial resources will not permit the building of a pipe-organ.

The answer must be tentative, since the development of electrones is proceeding so fast as perhaps to make any judgment here written in June 1958 out of date by the time the words appear in print. There are certain prior judgments, however, which can be made with confidence. The first is that the harmonium or American organ is death to decent church music, even of the simplest kind. Its tone is highly specialized, invariable, and very wearisome. If it be unprovided with pedals, it is necessarily utterly rhythmless; and if pedals are provided, the deep notes of the reeds are so disagreeable as to be valueless for rhythmical purposes. The judgment of Pope Pius X against the pianoforte in church is as downright as it is surprising:

> The employment of the piano is forbidden in church, as is also that of noisy or frivolous instruments such as drums, cymbals, bells and the like (*Catholic Church Music*, 1933, p. 10 par. 19).

With respect, we hold that a good piano is far better than an American organ for a small church, provided it be played with discretion, and provided the building be small enough not to damp too effectively the sound of the instrument.

Of the electrones, we would go so far as to say this: that any such instrument used in a church should be provided with two manuals and a full pedal board. Anything less than this will so hamper the organist's technique, and so restrict his already none

too varied repertory of music for voluntaries, as to make a reasonable offering of music unduly difficult. We would add that if an
electrone can be designed with a tonal decisiveness as effective as
that of a good well-balanced pipe-organ, and whose pedal department can provide something as effective as can be got from a well-
provided pedal department in pipes, there is nothing to be said
against it as an instrument for worship. But those who have the
planning of the musical appointments of new churches must take
great care, and must, if they are not among themselves adequately
equipped, take into consultation a musician of sufficient judgment,
to see that they are not deluded by purveyors of musical instruments which attempt to reproduce that 'organ atmosphere' which
in any case is not to our purpose in pipe-organs, and is certainly
offensive in electrones.

TEMPO

One of the points at which romanticism has unsuspectedly
overtaken English musicians of goodwill is in the matter of the
speed at which congregational music should be taken. In choral
music tempo is easily determined by the composers' indications or
the texture of the music. But in the rendering of congregational
hymns the matter of tempo is not infrequently interpreted by
reference more to temperament than to history.

Dr Vaughan Williams wrote in the Preface to the *English
Hymnal* (1906, page xiv), 'The present custom in English churches
is to sing hymns much too fast. It is distressing to hear *Nun
danket* or *St Anne* raced through at about twice the proper speed.'
Following out this expressed principle, he caused metronome
marks to be placed against every tune in that hymn book.

It was, apparently, the custom up to then to take hymns fairly
fast. This would be because the typical hymn tune of the 1861-
1906 era was the part-song, which did not in itself seem to demand
the dignity that a low speed always provides. But what is interesting is to ask what made that eminent editor (who, by the way,

was heard in 1956, on the fiftieth anniversary of the publication of his hymn book, to defend with characteristic pugnacity the whole policy of the book, in general and in detail) say that the 'proper speed' for those two hymn tunes, and for all hymn tunes, was slow.

It is impossible to be dogmatic about the speed at which primitive hymn tunes were sung. But there is no evidence that what we now call 'slow' was considered the correct speed for either the Lutheran chorales in their original form, or for psalm tunes. Take for example the most famous of Luther's tunes, *Ein' feste burg*. It is marked, in the Bach version, to be sung at minim 40 at EH 362 and 537, with the added direction, 'Very slow and solemn'. With the pauses as marked the tune according to the EH marking takes exactly two minutes to sing—say eight and a half minutes for the whole hymn. That is about the time occupied by a performance, with repeat, of the opening movement of Beethoven's *Pathétique* Sonata. Now the original of *Ein' feste burg* began thus:

10

A safe strong - hold our God___ is still

It is surely not a wild conjecture to assume that as sung in Luther's time it would have gone at minim 80 at least. But equally it is reasonable to mark the Bach version at a very low speed. Now it happens to have been Dr Vaughan Williams's conviction that the Bach versions of Lutheran chorales are incomparably superior to the originals. The *English Hymnal*, which has been so fruitful a source for the original versions of once-mutilated Genevan psalms, and for the introduction of old folk songs into hymnody, remained blind to what some of us are entitled to call the special virtues of the unbarred chorale; and one of its major contributions to English hymnody was the inclusion of 23 Bach settings within its covers. Of their intrinsic beauty there can be no doubt at all: but as a matter of historic fact it was the Bach chorale-version in his Cantatas and Passions that first set the fashion of very slow hymn singing. It remains debatable whether on ordinary occasions the versions of Lutheran tunes that he made to be sung one or (at most) two verses at a time in the course of his larger works make good vehicles for English hymns, especially when those hymns are of any length. I should personally judge that *Innsbruck* (EH 278) is, because of its essential simplicity, incomparable in the Bach version for 'The duteous day', the *Passion Chorale* for 'O sacred head', and *Ach gott und Herr* (329), because of the brevity of the hymn, equally appropriate to 'Strengthen for service' and that they should be taken slowly. *Ein' feste burg* (362) is ordinarily more singable when taken in a simpler version at at least twice the marked speed, and *Wachet Auf* (12) (marked at 39, taking for three verses the same time that *Ein' feste burg* takes for four) is intolerable for more than two verses, best with only one, except it be simplified. I should moreover venture the opinion that *Eisenach* (EH 138) is really far better in its original version

11

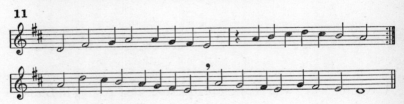

than in the Bach version as given in EH.

Anyhow, it was Bach who set the fashion for slow hymn-singing; pietism welcomed it, but it was also suitable for the context. Grandeur of that kind imported into ordinary Christian worship tends to introduce *disproportion*, and when it comes to marking a tune like *King's Lynn* (EH 562) as slow as 76, or *Nicaea* (EH 162) at 42, we may wonder whether this cult of slowness is not in itself a delusion of grandeur. Any slow movement (and a hymn tune is almost always technically a 'slow movement') gains dignity when it is made slower. It gains impressiveness—that must be the reason why Toscanini used to take the slow movement of the *Eroica* of Beethoven at 52. But we must beware of cultivating impressiveness. That is not always, as we have seen, conformable with the Gospel. A quick movement can express that understatement, that lack of pomp, which is suitable to Christian deportment, and that alertness which is proper to sons of the Resurrection. To judge by the depth of shock which good Christians commonly express when they notice an unusually quick movement imparted to a hymn tune, our habit is to be somewhat complacent in this, as in all other matters, in our handling of our music.

It is certainly the great virtue of plainsong hymn tunes that, at their simplest, they are entirely unassuming, and entirely uninterested in pomp. Whatever be the rights of this case—and it will certainly be hotly disputed—an affected slowness is psychologically an incitement to dignified languor, however noisily and ponderously the tune is rendered, and we should take care of this fact.

UNISON OR HARMONY

This at once raises the question whether, in congregational singing, unison or harmony should be the rule. Here opinions divide. Most English musicians follow Dr Vaughan Williams in preferring that the congregation sing in unison. But in Wales harmony is insisted on, and in many English congregations, and in almost all English choirs, the men prefer harmony partly because the melody often goes out of their range (for the average English voice is a lazy bass-baritone) and partly because it is beneath their dignity to sing what the women and boys are singing.

The angle from which we approach this is that suggested in our last few paragraphs. Singing in harmony, while it is surely agreeable to the texture of many four-part tunes, can be an incitement to languor—an occasion for dwelling on chords and giving notes their full value. The chief thing to be said for unison singing is surely that it is agreeable to fairly quick singing. (This point is not, of course, made in the *English Hymnal*, which prefers unison singing plus slow singing.)

Dietrich Bonhoeffer wrote thus about unison singing in *Life Together* (SCM, 1954, p. 50):

> Because it is bound wholly to the Word, the singing of the congregation, especially of the family congregation, is essentially singing in unison. Here words and music combine in a unique way. . . . The purity of unison singing, unaffected by alien motives of musical techniques, the clarity, unspoiled by the attempt to give musical art an autonomy of its own apart from the words, the simplicity and frugality, the humaneness and warmth of this way of singing is the essence of all congregational singing. . . . It becomes a question of a congregation's power of spiritual discernment whether it adopts proper unison singing.

There are several reasons why I believe that Englishmen should hesitate to take uncritically the advice of German authorities on musical matters; for one thing, the contempt of the typical modern Lutheran and Reformed pastor for any kind of organistic style or expression in playing hymns, and the manner in which sometimes this precept about unison singing is expressed, leave the impression that in Lutheran or Reformed hands music is very much a paid servant. For another, Lutheran practice has things made very easy for it by being far less international in its repertory of hymns than is English; it can therefore generalize more safely about the treatment of what it does sing. I find in certain phrases of Bonhoeffer as quoted above a tendency to sit down rather hard on any sign of musical 'autonomy', and this I believe to be less than neighbourly. But we may well learn from his main point. What are the objections to unison singing in any given congregation? Not theological, but always temperamental; too high for the men, too low for the women, none of them able to use their best notes, not so *interesting* as part-singing.

I believe that we shall not do much good by asking our congregations always to sing in unison all the hymns we print in our hymn books, or indeed many of them as they stand at present in conventional notation. It is, for example, an offence to the very texture of a tune like S. S. Wesley's *Hereford* (AM 329) to attempt to sing it in unison. *Hereford* is a tune which a German Lutheran would abominate, but which any Englishman with red blood in his veins must surely account beautiful and seemly. But I do believe that English hymn singing would be revolutionized if most of our hymn tunes were so printed as to suggest brisk unison singing, and the exceptional tune only were printed for use in harmony. The tradition behind the Lutheran tunes, the Genevan tunes, the French diocesan tunes and the psalm-tunes all the way to Wesley's day is of unison singing; and some of our finest modern tunes are explicitly so designed. Moreover, not a few Victorians whose harmony seems to lag are greatly improved by a new notation and light unison singing. There is a touch of what I mean in the arrangement of Barnby's tune *Laudes Domini* ('When morning gilds the skies') that is given in the *Clarendon Hymn Book* (no. 14). Two more examples are given on p. 98, which may be compared with their originals—one ancient, one from the nineteenth century.

It should be understood, of course, that the conventions of organ accompaniment ought in such a case to be comparable with those which govern the accompaniment of plainsong; that is, freedom of harmonic support should be discreetly exercised by the organist, with registration and phrasing appropriate to the texture of the tune, rather than a slavish following of a rigid four-part thump.

THE USE AND CHOICE OF HYMNS

Not infrequently one sympathizes with the well-known dictum of the late Bishop T. B. Strong, who complained that it would be to his liking if one hymn were sung every year, and that on Ash Wednesday, or with Professor C. S. Lewis's autobiographical remark, 'Hymns I have always hated'. Intemperance in their use is to be found in both anglican and nonconformist bodies. While it was the Dissenters who introduced hymn-singing techniques into

12 ABBEY
Unison
Melody, Scottish Psalter (1615)

cf. SP 492

13 Unison LONGWOOD
Con moto
J. Barnby

cf. CP 514 ii

English use on a large scale, it cannot now be said that they, who rely on hymns for so much that for anglicans is provided in the liturgy, are now the only offenders. A few years ago I played evensong at a parish church for a friend who was indisposed. It was the Sunday after Ascension, and in addition to the Canticles and a psalm and the other sung liturgical matter, the following hymns were sung (from EH):

427 Let all the world in every corner sing
141 Ascension office hymn (to the 'modern' tune, *Deus tuorum militum*)
420 Jesus shall reign
376 Come, let us join our cheerful songs
364 All hail the power of Jesus' name (seven verses)

together with the two hymns prescribed for use at Benediction. Not only was this a drastic overloading of the service, but the temper of every one of the tunes (that of the office hymn was, by accident, the heartiest of the French diocesan tunes) was exuberant. Apart from the opening hymn, none was very brief. (Hardly any hymn book in existence provides adequately for the liturgical need of short hymns of eight to twelve lines). The opening hymn, in the anglican office, was in any case unnecessary. There is no case whatever for the inclusion of more than three ordinary modern hymns in the anglican office with sermon. At the Eucharist the case is different, but a sense of decent restraint, with the main congregational emphasis at the Offertory and the Recessional, ought there to be observed.

It must be observed that although hymns of the modern kind (and plainsong office hymns imply a quite different kind of activity) are now regarded as necessary in anglican services for the congregation's benefit, they induce a habit of singing which, if it becomes the congregation's only habit, will damage them by throwing their public devotions out of balance. Hymns are traditionally sung with full voice, heartily. That is well. The Psalmist often urges it. But it is not well all the time. There is another

99

kind of singing, which both implies and fosters another kind of attitude, which a congregation neglects to its peril. Here the Dissenting traditions are obviously in the greatest danger: it has been classically said of Congregationalists (for example) that 'Hymns are their liturgy', and while that saying of Bernard Manning's has perhaps done good in arousing in that communion a sense of its responsibility in preserving a good heritage of hymnody, in the end it may turn out that it lays an emphasis on hymns which they were not, even for Dissenters, designed to bear, and that it implies too restricted a notion of what liturgy is. But anglican congregations have been affected quite deeply by the modern cult of hymns, and they, as much as anybody else, must not overlook the fact that as a congregation gets used to modern hymns, it begins to insist on them to the neglect of the proper singing of psalms, responses and other matter; and in the end its religious attitude becomes stiff, self-sufficient, unbiddable and arrogant.

It may also be said that one effective stimulus towards this corrupt attitude is the 'plugging' of certain hymn tunes which has become fashionable in our time. The damage done by the Glasgow Orpheus Choir under the direction of the late Sir Hugh Roberton not only in fostering a romantic and soulful attitude to hymns, but in 'popularizing' certain tunes, forms a respectable debit against their unquestionable credit in other musical matters. It was bad enough when the tune *Stracathro* (EH 445), in itself a singularly tender and beautiful melody, was thrust upon the listener with a resultant demand for it and insistence on its repetition that soon began to impose undue strain on its delicate aesthetic structure. With *Crimond*, a poorish tune in its own right, it was far worse. In the use of that tune, temperance has been entirely set aside. None but the most homespun of musical textures will stand up to such rough treatment. Textures which include a large measure of surface attractiveness are just those which will least stand up to it.

The cultivation of a less rigid, less hearty, less soulful form of hymn singing will quite certainly have good effect not only on performance and on piety, but on taste as well.

THE PSALMS: PLAINSONG AND ANGLICAN CHANTS

Another controverted matter on which we can throw light from our angle is the performance of psalms. There are broadly speaking two ways of regarding psalms. The first is to regard them as scripture read in concert; the second is to regard them as a kind of hymn.

As appointed in the Book of Common Prayer to be read in course through the month, the psalms are conceived in the former sense. Those communities which sustain the daily offices, and have not put away the complete reading of the psalms, have now found that in a general way plainsong is the serviceable medium. Plainsong in the Sarum form with which many Englishmen are now familiar is inward and undemonstrative: it is not rhetorical, and if there be accompaniment it is regarded as a solecism to make any gesture that will suggest rhetoric. Plainsong does very little more than keep the congregational utterance from falling into what the Presbyterian divines in the 1661 Prayer Book Colloquy called a 'confused murmure'. Plainsong moves at speaking speed, just slowly enough for the words to be properly formed and not, as they would otherwise be, mumbled; but certainly not slow enough to suggest declamation. Plainsong then physically corresponds to, and engenders, a certain humble and teachable attitude towards the psalms. There is in this tradition no thought of selecting the psalms more agreeable to Christian doctrine. This is the Old Testament, and we read it implicitly (this we imply in the *Gloria*) allowing that New Testament amplification or rebuke must be added.

At the other end of the scale we have the psalm treated as hymn: the extreme of this kind of practice is the metrical psalm, but in English churches the chanting of prose psalms, usually to anglican chants, is attempted. Now the anglican chant, though it has a tenuous formal connection with plainsong, belongs to the age of musical rhetoric. Anglican chants differ from one another in appropriateness to varying moods. They imply, in congregational use, the critical mind. They take a little longer to perform than plainsong, and they engage much more of the attention. It is a fact of experience that the 78th psalm to any anglican chant, or any combination of chants, seems much longer, because it becomes more rhetorically charged, than it does when sung to plainsong.

In cathedrals it is the custom to sing psalms to anglican chants (except when the absence of boys requires plainsong) without congregational participation. This produces a new effect—the effect of scripture read and, as it were, commented on. To listen to anglican chants thus rendered (or to the renderings made familiar in the daily broadcast services) is to be greatly edified, and psalm-singing becomes a *public* reading of scripture, as distinct from a *communal* reading of it.

These two kinds of music, then, represent different functions, and engender different attitudes It seems quite absurd to praise one and decry the other without these prior considerations. The case against anglican chants for congregational use is that, sung as they always are in harmony and with deliberation, they are difficult to fit to the natural rhythm of the words. But if psalms are regarded as hymns, selected from considerations of their consonance with received Christian doctrine and perhaps their convenient brevity, this does not seem to be a very weighty objection. False accents are tolerated by the dozen in hymns, and no less an authority than Robert Bridges declared himself content that for the sake of a good tune this should be so. Where psalms are sung by a trained choir they can be and often are rendered to anglican chants with exquisite faithfulness. But what is quite clear is that the 'inward' singing engendered by plainsong is a technique which any congregation needs to master, and that what is really objectionable in the congregational rendering of anglican chants is not so much the accidental false emphasis as the horrible incongruity of hearty, arrogant singing with the reading of Scripture. Congregations and their directors are then advised to consider the relative merits of (*a*) reading psalms in course to plainsong as a personal discipline; (*b*) hearing psalms sung to good chants by a good choir as scripture interpreted, and (c) singing psalms, or selections from them, as hymns with what approximation to decent rhythm they can compass. They should be warned against bawling the psalms in any case. But whatever happens, congregations should not be denied the opportunity of knowing and making their own this priceless treasury of human devotion, imperfections, errors and all.

For completeness we may mention a use of the psalms which is familiar to anglicans—the use of selected verses in Introits and other liturgical material at the Eucharist. This use is highly significant and profitable, but it has no musical significance beyond what we have already said, since it is almost invariably associated with plainsong.

But we may add as a postscript that where psalms are used as hymns, a version of the psalter that treats their text as a hymn book treats the texts of hymns is tolerable and even desirable. Most selective psalters are unsatisfactory because their editors so often have quaint notions of what will offend their people. But the gesture made by the *Broadcast Psalter* in providing explanatory headings and informed emendations of the English text is, for this kind of purpose, one to be warmly welcomed.

GÉLINEAU

One new technique of psalmody which it would be churlish to pass without mention here is the psalmody of Père Gélineau, which has come into use in Roman Catholic circles on the Continent, and of which a selective English version has been prepared for English use. The Protestant community at Taizé uses this form of psalmody in its daily offices, but it is primarily a device to bring back the psalms into Catholic use, from which in effect, apart from the monastic offices, they have so long disappeared.

Gélineau's technique is to provide a very simple but significant phrase, or a pair or triplet of phrases, and arrange his translation in that its stresses correspond faithfully with the bar-lines of the phrase. One note of the phrase normally fills a bar, and the bar is divided in terms of minims and crotchets to accommodate the syllables within it. It is not a speech-rhythm technique, and its tempo is not, as in anglican chanting, elastic; it can be used either in unaccompanied harmony or in accompanied unison, and antiphons are provided for the psalms. It has nothing to offer that cannot be got from a well-pointed psalter: but its effect in performance is unusual and, at first, highly impressive. Its real significance is as a Catholic gesture, and it is already in use in Catholic homes as well as in churches. Fortunately, Père Gélineau is a musician with an uncanny gift for composing a phrase of a few notes which is musically suggestive. The harmonic conventions are modern and sometimes startling, and it falls nearer to the anglican chant than to plainsong if we would place it by reference to the principles we stated earlier.[1]

THE FOLK MASS

Father Geoffrey Beaumont's *Folk Mass* (Weinberger, 1957) has aroused, through a presentation on television and through the publicity given to it especially by its detractors, an interest which, while we would not wish to judge the work negligible, has become disproportionate. It remains to be seen whether a reader of this page in ten years' time, should there be any such, will be aware of the work to which we here refer, or whether we are speaking of a landmark in the history of English church music.

The present writer was privileged to review the work before publication in the *British Weekly* of 30 December, 1956, and although that review was written before hearing any performance of the music, his opinions have not substantially altered.

[1] See the publications of The Grail (58 Sloane Street, S.W.1) as follows: *Twenty-four Psalms and a Canticle* (melodies only: 1955); *Accompaniments and Four-part Harmonies* to the above book (1956); *Cinquante-Trois Psaumes et Quatre Cantiques* (originally published by Editions du Cerf, Paris, in French: melodies only); and a gramophone record, 10 inch LP, GR24 (30s. 11½d.) on which eight of the psalms are sung in various ways by choirs of monks and children. The record is extremely impressive.

The Folk Mass is a setting of the sung portions of the anglican Eucharist in an idiom suggesting what is compendiously and inaccurately known as 'jazz'. Such idioms, in rhythm and melody, as are heard in the tango, the fox-trot and the beguine are worked into the structure of each number. At two points, in the hymns associated with it and in a chorus which is used for certain Amens, for the Sanctus, and for the doxologies of the Gloria and the Lord's Prayer, the idiom is what might better be called 'music hall'; indeed the tune in question is very strongly reminiscent of the leading theme in Eric Coates's incidental music to *The Dam Busters*.

The intention, as is now well known, was to write a Mass setting in what today, in the composer's view, corresponds to the folk music of the middle ages, so that the people who are wedded culturally to the civilization represented by this kind of dance music and light music might be made to feel at home in church. It is, as it were, one more effort to 'take the church to the people' in the name of the Lord.

Such an aim is commendable, but while we may dismiss charges of blasphemy as fantastic, and while we may not wish to castigate the work so violently as did Dr Greenhouse Allt in that same lecture from which we quoted his views on the Bishop of Leicester's theories of church music (Hinrichsen, op. cit., pp. 50f.), it may be permissible to offer two comments.

In the first place, I believe Dr Allt to be right in saying that Father Beaumont has, despite his excellent intentions, misconceived the nature of 'folk music'. The consequence of this is to be seen in the comment which has fairly frequently been made by those whose interests and information in the world of jazz and light music are extensive, that the jazz-element in the Mass is already out of date. That may be a comment of the expert, to which Father Beaumont would reply that it is of no consequence, because the people to whom he hopes to minister are themselves that much out of date, and are not necessarily keeping up with the latest developments in that field. None the less, it may be doubted whether idioms so ephemeral can be called 'folk music'. For folk song is not simply what everybody sings. It presupposes certain habits of transmission; I believe it strictly presupposes oral transmission and a complete absence of that commercialism which artificially induces the popularity of 'jazz'. It presupposes improvisation on and amplification of traditional tunes and songs, but not the discarding of them after a year or two.

For that reason I believe that the only part of the Folk Mass that is anything like folk song is the 'Dam Busters' passage, and the hymns. Here we have real humanity, here we have an anchor with a past for the moment not repudiated. 'Lord, thy word abideth' is a magnificent tune, full-blooded but not pretentious, suitable for congregational unison singing, and admirably constructed by a composer whose gift for melody is stunted in the hectic short phrases of the rest of the composition. The two other hymns that appear in the Paxton recording of the Mass (Paxton LPR201) are almost equally good.[1] That, just because it is 'music hall' rather than 'dance band', is a tolerable notion of folk song.

But my other observation, which recapitulates what I wrote in the *British Weekly* nearly two years ago, is that this notion of evangelism is misconceived. For Father Beaumont has not sufficiently considered how far this music deliberately partakes of the corruption of the world out of which he would redeem people, and how far it transcends it. To most ears it appears to be positively tainted with that corruption—the corruption of arrogance, carelessness, impatience and even fear. Its characteristic obsessions with short phrases alternating with abrupt changes to new phrases, its hypnotic rhythms which are not rhythms but metrical patterns (except at one point, at 'We praise thee' in the *Gloria*, where a real rhythmic ambiguity appears with excellent effect)—these things do not suggest redemption. They suggest acceptance where the church should be saying 'No'. The Folk Mass brings back quite starkly the question of evangelism in the

[1] An alternative recording is Oriole MG20019. There a small orchestra is used.

form, 'How far may the church go to meet the people?' In the Paxton recorded version the worst is made of it by the employment of a theatre-organist playing a Hammond organ and a close-harmony quartet with a cantor who comes perilously near to crooning at several points. The rougher justice of a skiffle-band may well be a better fate for it. But at present I am not persuaded that the enterprise, considered as missionary work, is sound, for it appears to have some of the defects of end-gaining, effect-hunting and a desire for quick influence that have brought plenty of similar evangelical adventures to grief.

CHAPTER ELEVEN

INTERIM CONCLUSION

OUR contention then can be summed up in these propositions:

(1) That the relation of service in which music stands to the church should be one of free and cheerful service, such as is agreeable to the Kingdom, not of servitude.

(2) That the makers and performers of music in church must especially beware of the sins of pride and greed and the derived error of doing and thinking what is not conformable with good doctrine.

(3) That this 'good doctrine' teaches us of the intimate relation between the Church and Christ, through his Incarnation, Passion and Resurrection, and is waiting for daily expression in all forms of church-behaviour, of which music is one form.

(4) That the criticism of church music in practice should proceed from the ground of doctrine, should avoid facile legalism, and should be constructive enough to encourage the good, before being repressive enough to ensure the avoidance of error.

When all is said, the musician in the church is an artist, and the fact, brought out in chapter 3 above, that he shares so many of the natural presuppositions that underlie Christian doctrine, should be used as a means of reconciliation between him and the church. There is no need, on any doctrinal ground, to talk of the artist's autonomy in terms which suggest that he wishes for no neighbourly relations with any other field of discourse: but neither is there any need for Christians to take a high-handed and uncompassionate attitude towards the artist's sense of personal vocation.

We do not therefore plead here for patronage. Such patronage as is being revived in a modern fashion by certain enlightened churches must be welcomed as an act of generosity and as a means for the adornment of the Gospel. But patronage suggests the gracious granting of a temporary freedom to the artist to do his work unhampered either by the economic insecurity which would otherwise distract him, or by much uninformed criticism. A Christian community can be generous in patronage and still philistine, taking an attitude of leaving the distinguished Mr X to paint his picture or compose his Mass without doing more for him than protecting him from those distractions or controversies or inconveniences which would otherwise make him unwilling to paint or write. What we look for rather is what must be expressed, for want of better words than these somewhat hackneyed ones, as partnership and encounter.

Near the end of his book, *Choir of Muses* (Sheed & Ward, 1953), Étienne Gilson writes:

> No one is humbler than the artist before his art, even if he is vain before men. He is even humble about his life, which is, he is aware, different from other lives. He asks by what unmerited grace he should be called from among so many. This feeling goes so deep that when he is among men engrossed by the needs of ordinary life modesty will not let him speak of his own way of living. He hides it as the saint hides his life of prayer which can be talked about only among saints (p. 183).

The title of the chapter in which those words appear is 'The Artist and the Saint', and Professor Gilson has just been examining the recorded sayings of certain artists, including Sibelius, Ramuz, Oscar Wilde and Gide, which indicate a reaching out towards a 'Gospel aesthetic'. This 'Gospel aesthetic' he describes as 'very bad theology' (p. 182), and as there expressed that is what it certainly is. But why should it remain so?

The minister of religion and the artist ought to look at each other with great sympathy. What minister of religion but would agree that something of the above quotation chimes with his own inner experience? Ministers, like artists, are commonly individualists; not infrequently temperamental, sensitive and at times impatient. There is much that goes on in their lives that can be 'talked about only among saints'; but among the saints they can, if they will, number the artists.

And we are here dealing not with Ramuz and Sibelius, but with the journeyman organist and the hack-composer. It does not matter. They too are artists; they should at once abandon their work if they are not. They too have a sense of vocation which presents itself as something piercing at least as often as it presents itself as something pious.

It will remain bad theology so long as the theologian and the artist refuse to communicate with one another; as long as the theologian regards the artist as fundamentally a temperamental trifler, and the artist the theologian as an obstinate and ignorant theorist, the best we shall get is patronage from church to music, together with tentative moralisms from musicians to musicians. At worst it will be, as it often in practice is, a wicked waste of an opportunity for glorifying God through fruitful partnership. Men, as men, are bound together in the body of humanity, and in the body of Christ. Where they accept with penitent gratitude their common humanity, and rejoice together in their common Christ-hood, the work of the Lord will be done. It will be done nowhere else.

SPECIFICATION OF THE ORGAN IN UNIVERSITY COLLEGE CHAPEL, OXFORD

Two manuals and pedals.

Pedal organ

1 Bourdon	. .	16
2 Quint	. . .	$10\frac{2}{3}$
3 Principal	. .	8
4 Flöte	. . .	8
5 Fifteenth	. .	4
6 Octave Flöte	. .	4
7 Superoctave	. .	2
8 Cromhorne	. .	16
9 Cromhorne octave	.	8

Great organ

10 Open Diapason	.	8
11 Stopped Diapason	.	8
12 Dulciana	. .	8
13 Principal	. .	4
14 Rohrflöte	. .	4
15 Fifteenth	. .	2
16 Mixture (19, 22, 26)		III

Swell Organ

17 Double gedeckt (to tenor C)	.	16
18 Gedeckt	. . . .	8
19 Spitzflöte	. . . .	8
20 Gedeckt octave	. . .	4
21 Spitz octave	. . . .	4
22 Gedeckt Twelfth	. . .	$2\frac{2}{3}$
23 Gedeckt superoctave	. .	2
24 Spitz superoctave	. . .	2
25 Spitz 22nd	. . . .	1
26 Sesquialtera (12, 17)	. .	II
27 Sesquialtera (19, 24)	. .	II
28 Cromhorne	. . . .	16
29 Cromhorne octave	. . .	8
Tremulant		

Couplers: Swell-Great, Swell-Pedal, Great-Pedal: Great and Pedal
Combinations

Accessories: Four pistons to each department
Reversible pistons, Swell-Great and Great-Pedal couplers
Balanced Swell pedal
Double touch cancel on stop keys

The organ was built in 1953 by J. W. Walker & Son of Ruislip, in consultation with the organist, Mr John Webster. The Swell organ is built from ranks of pipes (Gedeckt, Spitz and Cromhorne) plus the sesquialtera, and occupies a very small space. A descriptive article on this organ will be found in *The Organ*, no. 148 (April, 1958, pp. 191ff.).

INDEXES

I. SCRIPTURE REFERENCES

I Cor.		*Phil.*	
3.22-23	41	2.5ff.	21
		3.10	54
II Cor.		*Col.*	
5.17	71	3.16	23
Eph.		*Rev.*	
1.15ff.	53f.	11.15	38
5.19	23	21.5	71

II. BOOKS

III. HYMN TUNES

(with numbers in EH where applicable)

Abbey, 98
Ach Gott und Herr (*329*), 94
'At the Feast' (*Sankey*), 72

Bishopthorpe (*408*), 67
'By and by' (*Bliss*), 73

Carlisle (*236*), 67
Carolyn, 77
Christchurch, (*411*), 76
Crimond, 78, 100

David's Harp (*378*), 76
Down Ampney (*152*), 76

Ein Feste Burg, (*362*), 93f.
Eisenach (*138*), 94
Engelberg, 65, 75
Eventide (*363*)

Green Hill, 67

Hambledon, 77
Herald (*205*), 67
Hereford, 97
Herongate (*597*), 59n.

Innsbruck (*278*), 94

King's Lynn (*562*), 59n., 94

Laudes Domini, 97
Longwood, 98
'Lord, thy Word abideth' (*Beaumont*), 106

Monks Gate (*402*), 59n.

Nicaea (*162*), 94
Nun Danket (*533*), 92

Passion Chorale, 48, 94

Richmond (*375*), 67

Sagina, 75
St Andrew of Crete, 67
St Anne (*450*), 92
St Crispin (*246 App.*), 70
St Mary (*84*), 65
Sherston, 77
Stracathro (*445*), 100
Surrey (*491*), 67
Sussex (*385*), 59n.

Thornbury (*545*), 65, 75

University (*93*), 76

Wachet Auf (*12*), 94
Winchester Old (*30*), 76

117

IV. MUSIC

V. PERSONS AND SUBJECTS